# On My Way

DEWHURST
Enterprises LTD.

# On My Way

*Bond Girl     Scream Queen*

written by Martine Beswicke
with
Simon Firth

Foreword by John Logan

Designed by Martijn Mulder
Edited by Christian Winter & Martijn Mulder

ISBN: 9781399996587

Published by

# DEWHURST
*Enterprises* LTD.

# On My Way

*Bond Girl*      *Scream Queen*

Martine Beswicke

Foreword by

John Logan
Screenwriter for Skyfall, SPECTRE, Gladiator, The Aviator

# CONTENTS

# 1

## FOREWORD
### BY JOHN LOGAN

---

Director Peter Brook ends his seminal study of theatre THE EMPTY SPACE with these four words: "A play is play."

Those words kept echoing in my head as Martine Beswicke led me through her life in this wonderful and witty book. Here is a woman who enjoys her life, who savors friends, who collects adventures, who never steps away from a challenge, who embraces risk, who laughs boldly, who plays.

She's a Wild Child, she's a Cinema Legend, she's a Bond Girl, she's a Scream Queen, she's a Sex Symbol, she's a Survivor. And maybe that last is what echoes the most for me. Martine has survived in an industry that discards women recklessly, that can be cruel and calculating, that so often eats its young. As you'll read, it wasn't always an easy or straightforward journey for her. The road was twisting and treacherous and Martine made her share of mistakes. She fell hard, but she got back up. Always with a sense of her own worth and dignity.

When I look at those films that launched her career – FROM RUSSIA WITH LOVE, THUNDERBALL, ONE MILLION YEARS BC, PREHISTORIC WOMEN and DR. JEKYLL AND SISTER HYDE – I see a shockingly modern presence. She transcends the limitations of some of these films, and later ones, to create a unique genre icon: Martine the Great and Powerful. You can practically hear her roaring from the celluloid. She banishes timidity. There are no safe choices. She struts. Martine utterly owns her sexuality, her mixed-race heritage, her humor, her power, her body. She's no one's victim, she's no one's plaything. Martine went through a deep dive into sex-and-drugs-and-rock-and-roll and emerged with that imperious head held high and that wicked smile still vibrant. And with something else as well, with the kind of wisdom that only comes with a life fully lived.

Thank goodness she's been good enough to tell us her story. I hope you enjoy it as much as I did. Now, go play with Martine.

JL

JOHN LOGAN received the Tony award for his play *Red*. As a screenwriter, he has been three times nominated for the Oscar™ and has received Golden Globe, BAFTA, WGA and Edgar awards. His film work includes *Skyfall, Gladiator, The Aviator, Hugo, Rango, Sweeney Todd, Spectre, They/Them, The Last Samurai,* and *Any Given Sunday.* He created the television series *Penny Dreadful* for Showtime.

# 2

# PREFACE

## "OUT OF MANY, ONE PEOPLE"

There is in Jamaica a motto. It is, "Out of many, One People".

Jamaica was originally home to the Arawaks but due to the plundering of the island by Europeans, they were massacred. The slave trade movement introduced Africans and later worker immigration from the Indian sub-continent such as China and Syria. Together with the English, Spanish and Portuguese, this resulted in a melting pot of all races whereby now, when two Jamaicans reproduce within a family, one can never be sure what the skin colours might be. But the result is one Jamaican people. No matter the various backgrounds, Jamaicans become united despite possible skin colour differences within a family. The motto is to remind the populace that they should be one, and not divided, and which has contributed to a pride that creates an interesting and unique island population.

And so too is our family very much a part of the multi coloured family. There is a rumour that my great-great grandfather married a slave; this was something that happened throughout the time and the land. Within their family, all their children were different colours, and it also perpetuated through the future generations. My sister is brown, I am white and yet we look alike. My father was white with dark hair, his sister white and blue eyed. People look at me and say, 'You're not black, how come you are Jamaican.' I say, 'That's why we are Out of Many One.'

Out of subsequent interest I took a DNA test to look into my lineage. I have in me a wide heritage: Portuguese, African, Irish and Scottish.

# 3

# INTRODUCTION

---

I was lying on a beautiful beach, sunning myself in my bikini. My feet were playing with the glistening white sand and dipping into the waters' edge of the warm Caribbean Sea's gentle waves. The colours and scents around me were magical and all was framed by coconut trees and the moving fronds of the flora touched by the soft sweet breeze.

I had been brought from London to The Bahamas on an aeroplane that had been chartered for the entire cast and crew of a film. I was to play an island girl, and while I actually am an island girl, the combination of the UK weather and my London nightlife choices had not served me well. I was too white, and I was too thin.

In much the same way as the rest of the film crew were instructed for the fresh day's work by way of a Call Sheet, I too was given a Call Sheet for my specific job of work which was to sun myself on the beach and to eat heartily. The beach was called Love Beach, and the island was New Providence.

I was in The Bahamas for eight weeks' work; six week's filming and two weeks' 'preparing'. 'How fabulous was this,' I thought. Love Beach was a private beach at the time. The film crew had taken over the beach to film a love scene of sorts between the two principal actors. One of the reasons I was so thin was because of all the dancing I did in the London clubs. There had never at the time been any necessity for diets or gyms due to my nights of mad and creative dancing.

The day's dining was fully catered for by the film set. The evening champagne was fully catered for by the film's director.

I was 23. I had done two films, three TV episodes, and some modelling. The year was 1965, the director was Terence Young, the stars were Sean Connery, Claudine Auger and Luciana Paluzzi. And the film was *Thunderball*.

If this was an early indication of where a film career was heading, what else might Life have to afford me? But really, how did I manage to find myself here?

# 4

## 1941–1954

# JAMAICA, CHILDHOOD

---

■ **MUMMY**

With regard to marriage and children, I was always dubious as to whether my mother was following her dream or whether she was following a sense of protocol. Myrtle May Penso Beswick was born in 1912 and didn't marry until she was 29. She had me when she was 30. For that era, getting married at 29 and giving birth in her 30s was quite late. I had no idea why she married late. Maybe it had something to do with the fact she was adventurous. Even though she was very attached to her family, a part of her was always independent.

She was beautiful, very elegant, and very upright; this last was something she instilled in me. If I was stooping, she would put me against the wall and say, 'Watch your posture, stand up straight.' Her posture was superb. My mother worked for her father in his various businesses. He had a fabric store, two gas stations, and two estates; one in the country, and one in Kingston. Hers was a very affluent and well-respected family.

As a teenager and in her early twenties, she was athletic and adventurous. She was an excellent team hockey player. Her father bought her a horse, Serenity, which she rode on her father's extensive Kingston Estate. She loved to ride. She was very proud of her horse; she was an elegant looking rider with the full Jodhpur outfit. I however never rode a horse except when my father would take me on a horse; that was the limit of my exposure and interest.

A highlight of her adventures was hiking to the top of the Blue Mountains at night with a group of women to camp and to welcome the sunrise the following morning. Blue Mountains peaked at 2256m. One could not get to the top in a car; the only way was on foot with the aid of pack mules for the transportation of supplies. It was a hard hike. Perhaps they also had the Jamaican equivalent of Sherpas to help with the climb and the set up. When they got to the top, they set up camp. And the following morning, they saw the sunrise. I am thinking this must have taken a couple of days; the climb the night before, a camp overnight, the sunrise, and then to descend the day of the sunrise. She must have been in her early 20s when she did this. Why does this appear as a highlight of her early life for me? Well, it was always a story she told me, many times. I was very proud of her journey up the Blue Mountain; it must not have been at all easy. I admire her for doing it; I have a great deal of respect for her.

Her independence was a huge part of her life and I think this is something that she passed on to me at a very early age. I always had a sense of pride for her journey, especially as it happened in the late 1930s.

Later in life, she bought and sold property, she painted; it was all very much a part of her nature. However, that contrasted with her devotion to Christianity. She went to church every Sunday, she knew the bible, and really, I believe this provided for her a form of balance; a balance that made her fair and strong. As a mother to me, she would ask, 'Why don't you want to go to church?' 'Not my thing Darling,' I would reply. Mummy was a devout Christian, her trust in God was total and which, to her eternal disappointment, was also not passed on to me. Her faith was unswerving and I can say she was the best Christian I have ever known. Every Sunday would see her go to church, she knew and quoted her bible, and she said her prayers. She was hopeful of my conversion and I did go through the Communion process, but both my cousin and I were not that involved in the church. However, as we were the eldest, there were times when we had to attend the meetings, say the prayers, and take the bread and the wine. It was an education I was faced with until I was in my mid-teens when I was finally able to say no.

When her marriage to Daddy fell apart, and while she never remarried, my mother had boyfriends, both in Jamaica, and later in London, and then again when back in Jamaica. I was happy for her. Many children can be upset if their mother has anyone else. I never understood that thinking; I was just really happy for her. When she would go away for weekends with her boyfriends, our house keeper, Zelpha, was in charge and she was really a part of the family.

And the boyfriends were all lovely to us and certainly made her happy.

## ■ DADDY

Ronald Stuart Beswick was my father. He was born in Jamaica but descended from English and African heritage. We heard that his great grandfather hailed from England and owned a plantation. This was at a time whereby, to work the land, the plantation owners owned and managed slaves, which included women and children. It was a well-known occurrence that the plantation owners would take a slave girl as their lover resulting in offspring. Rumour has it that my great-great grandfather actually married his slave girl but, we don't really have the proof.

My father was a Busha who managed plantations. They called him Busha Beswick. Bushas manage the running of the estate and the workers on behalf of the plantation owner. At the time I was born, he was a manager of a Port Antonio plantation.

He was a really handsome man; almost the Errol Flynn or Clark Gable of the family. I never really knew him as well as I might have done had he not gone away to work so often.

Daddy however was the bad boy of the family. He liked his highballs; he liked a bit of gambling and he liked the ladies. The gambling was not based in a casino as there weren't any casinos in Jamaica at that time. He and his friends would set up poker games, rotating the hosting between their various houses. I remember a sense of the men setting up the table and then pouring their rum and coke highballs. The gambling was not high stakes, but it was enough to cause issues at home. The conflict would have come from the fact my mother's father was helping to support and provide for us. Her family was more affluent than his parents so it might not have sat right with Mummy and her father that the support could have included that of gambling. I knew there was a conflict between my parents as it wasn't to her liking; the men, the drinking, the gambling. Although I never saw Daddy drunk, he could become quite argumentative and opinionated after a few.

But it was not just my father that exhibited this behaviour. The whole Beswick family was a little scandalous. We would later hear that both he and his brother had several children outside of marriage. I have an older half-sister, Pat Haughton-James, who lives in the USA and who I am still in touch with. With the famous Beswicke 'turned up' nose, we look very much alike. She was born before my

14

Mummy and Daddy

15

Mummy and Mary Rose

parents were married. Later when he went to the Dominican Republic, and when his marriage to my mother fell apart, he later remarried and had a further five children. All in all, he had nine children - that we know of! God knows, when he went to work in America for awhile, maybe he left a few offspring there too.

## MEETING AND MARRYING

I have no idea how my mother and father met each other, or where. I had asked her for her story but she was shy in the forthcoming and telling. I have the feeling their meeting and marrying was an instant thing, maybe kind of naughty, but I never found out. This was 1930s Jamaica, under British rule and British governors, with British politics. While on the one hand there was propriety, on the other, there was not. Maybe Mummy's religion had a part to play in their marriage. They got married in Mummy's Church in St Andrew. Her father, her family, they were all Catholic. It was assumed my mother would also be Catholic, but against her family's wishes she made the decision to be Protestant. The wedding reception was held at Drominagh, also in St Andrew.

However, on September 26, 1941, Myrtle May Penso Beswick gave birth to me, Mary Rose Penso Beswick, in the Port Antonio Hospital, Jamaica. I assume my father was in attendance at the event as they were newly married and both 30 years old. I say 'in attendance', I am sure he was probably pacing and smoking waiting for the birth of his first born with May.

My parents, Ronald and May, were a very handsome couple; both tall and regal. I always thought they looked like movie stars in their wedding picture but their union was definitely a case of opposites attracting. I never saw them dance or being intimate or kissing in company. My mummy was a Christian and he was a bit of a rogue.

I believe however they were very definitely in love; for a while anyway. Even at a young age the feeling I had was that sex was a big part of their relationship. Upon reflection however, perhaps I was surmising that they were in love because they were merely together, and because they were such a good-looking pair. They were together until I was eight.

## PORT ANTONIO

I was born in Port Antonio when my parents were already living in a house. I cannot say where the house was, nor remember its name, but we were there for only a few months.

17

I remember later when I was in my 30s, I had returned home for a couple of weeks and I was in north Jamaica sitting at Frenchman's Cove in Port Antonio. It was the site of a fabulous hotel that had a river running through it. A man in his 80s saw me and approached me. Friendly and wizened, he asked me; 'How you do today girl? You want a coconut water?' 'Yes, that would be great.'

As he returned with the coconut, he said,
'I recognise you!'
'How come, we never meet.'
'Because you look just like your father, Busha Beswick who I worked for. And he was the best Busha I ever knew. And I know where him bring you home. Come mek a show you, is jus' up de hill.'

He led the way up the hill above the beach from where I had been previously sitting. When we reached the top, I looked out to a view over the sea. Framing the view were bougainvillea bushes and fruit trees; it was this image that I had been carrying in my head for years of a family home. I must have seen that view as a baby, and without knowing why, it had stuck in my brain, unconnected to anything until the old man took me to the place of what I knew then was my first home. It was absolutely mind blowing.

## ALBION

When I was still a baby, we all moved to Albion. It was my grandfather's estate house and plantation estate in the county of St Thomas, 18 miles from Kingston. Grandfather decided my father would be the Busha for Albion. He was installed to oversee the plantation of cattle, bananas and vegetables. There were two houses on the estate. There was a Great House and the Busha's house. I am not sure if I can put a name to the design of the Busha's house but my memory of it was a simple wooden and stilted structure built above a large cellar. There was a covered veranda which ran the full length of the house. It was furnished with several rocking chairs and screens that provided protection against mosquitos. The grounds were lush; there was a wide variety of fruit trees, vegetables and livestock which our live-in servants cared for. They also cared for us.

Although there was a car, Daddy rode his horse to work on the plantation and sometimes, Daddy's girl got a special treat and rode with him.

## DROMINAGH

I was four years old when we moved to Drominagh. It was situated at 37

Eastwood Park Road in Kingston. Drominagh to this day holds a very special place in my heart. It was magical. It was my grandfather's house and it was a beautiful property. It had a low stone wall surrounding the 27-acre property. The entrance to the property had a driveway which split into two so you could drive around and back out again. It formed a heart-like shape and at the driveway's split stood an old canon. The house was supposedly built by slaves so it might have been considered to be a Great House. The front stairs led up to a veranda which ran the full width of the house. The living room held a grand piano; the dining room had heavy mahogany tables, chairs and cases filled with an abundance of glass and dinner ware for all the entertaining. Either side of the hallway were the bedrooms and bathrooms. There were two further rooms; one of which stored yet more crockery, and the other was a private kitchen used exclusively by my step grandmother, Aunt Zelia, for her baking delights. There was a walkway that led to the large main kitchen where the cooks created all the meals.

The name Drominagh is apparently Irish. The house sat on many acres of land and was primarily a farm with cows, horses, chickens, turkeys, pigeons (a favourite of Grandfather's) and pigs. There was also an extensive vegetable garden and many exotic fruit trees, including mangoes which were everyone's favourite. We were allowed to pick and eat most of the fruit except two types of mangoes which were my grandfather's very specific favourites. This was big Daddy's law and that which was to be forever obeyed.

## CROSSROADS

We moved to a small house in the Crossroads district of Kingston, a little further away from Drominagh. We rented it. I have no idea why we moved but I think my parents must have voluntarily moved us, perhaps for easier school access. I do know my grandfather was not happy about us renting.

## RETURN TO DROMINAGH

When Daddy had moved to the Dominican Republic and my parents' marriage fell apart, my Mummy and I moved back to the Drominagh estate. Her father gave her a piece of land on which he built her a house of her choosing. She designed the house and she got the workers in to build it; she really did the whole thing. I remember standing there watching the workers map out the plan of the house with string. The foundations were then dug and the house was built and magically, we had a lovely new home with a badminton court, vegetable garden and some space for some chickens and pigs. She was remarkable. We were once again a part of the Penso Estate. With the Drominagh Main House in the middle, we were on

19

the left, and our cousins, who seemed more like our brothers to us, were on the right. We all had a wonderful freedom to play together in the extensive grounds of Drominagh.

I truly loved this property and I was horrified when I found out it had been sold to later be knocked down. It was replaced with a cement block for the Halfway Tree Primary School. Even now, it hurts. I cannot find any photos of the house or the grounds.

## ■ PRESCHOOL

My first actual memory was welcoming my baby sister into the world, Laurellie Ann Penso Beswick. She was born on 3rd December 1943. I was given a little green rocking chair made by a Beswick uncle. Laurellie was a baby and I was two years old. I was inspired to take my sister out of her crib and to rock her and to sing to her. In order to get her out of the crib, I had to pull the side of the crib down; it was made of a very heavy metal. I picked her up. My parents arrived and they were shocked; absolutely horrified. How the hell did I manage to release the crib side? I could have dropped her. What went through my parents' minds? And then, not learning any lesson, I did it again! I believe these two moments were the beginning of the free-thinking wild child I later became. My poor parents.

I discovered ants to be a favourite taste treat. To this day I still retain the taste memory of the acid crunch; delicious. I was three, everything went in my mouth. It is what a child does, everything goes in their mouth. I don't think this is abnormal. But why ants? I cannot say. Today, in some parts of the world they are considered a delicacy, even if that example of insect treat is cooked, or sugar coated. Me, I squished them and put them in my mouth. We also had many fruit trees, of which one was a jimbilin tree. The fruit of that tree had that same acidic crunch and taste, so I didn't stop eating the fruit or the ants. That said, ants were my favourite. I have since refined my culinary preferences.

I was a tree climber; sometimes I climbed without clothes. I have no idea why I climbed like that, the freedom perhaps; I just felt it was nice to remove my clothes. To this day, I do not know how I climbed without hurting myself.

I had a doll; it was almost as big as I was and together, we went on adventures. On one such adventure I even managed to get on a county bus. The bus passed our house on a country road; it was the only type of public transport in this area for the workers to go to town and to the market. As the community was made up of workers on the plantations, I was spotted. I was recognised as Busha Beswick's daughter and I was returned unharmed. Again, with no lesson learned, I repeated the efforts a couple more times.

In our estate, there was a Busha house that had a walled pool that was secured with a locked gate. The presence of a pool was one of the perks of being a Busha. The gate was not locked when the family went for a swim. For whatever was going through my mind, I undressed and tried and failed to bypass the locked gate. So, I left my clothes at the gate and went off to my favourite mango tree in another part of the estate to climb it and cloud watch. I would lie in the Y of some branches and look through the leaves to marvel at the clouds. I do not recall how my parents found me but seeing the discarded clothes near the pool gate, they must have thought that I had possibly got into the water and drowned. As I have said, poor Mummy and Daddy.

The second event was more serious. This took place in a wash house where the laundry was done. There was a round stove, quite big and filled with burning coals. Old fashioned, huge and heavy clothes irons were placed on the stove to heat up. Our maid was ironing. When the ironing had been finished, or the irons had lost their useful heat, they were put on one side and out of the way. As I had my own little play iron, I decided to put it in the fire. Fearful of the danger, the maid pushed me away from the stove, but I fell back and into stove. I burned one leg, badly. Upon my parents arriving to the screams, my mother had to physically restrain my father from attacking the maid. Daddy had to drive 18 miles of county roads to Kingston with his seriously injured daughter who was crying and screaming in pain. I have no idea what happened to the maid, but she really did try to save me.

Mummy and Daddy came to a decision to curtail my wanderings and a pink leather harness became a part of my daily wardrobe. They didn't let go of it either. Although essential to my safety and their peace of mind, I do believe this had a life-long effect on my desire for freedom. In other words, 'Don't fence me in.' I wore it until I outgrew it. I became tall, I was big footed. This was from when I was four or five. With the harness now discarded and not replaced, I re-found my freedom. I again took up my wanderings. For the most part, they were usually undertaken just within the estate.

I am not sure whether the mishap with the iron was the final straw because the family moved to Kingston and into the Family Estate, Drominagh, where there were other family members to support Mummy and Daddy with their wild child. Clearly it was a time for education and hopefully long-term safety. However, not before I had had my final escape before school education began.

I took a long walk and found and boarded a local tram. I was about a mile away from home when I climbed aboard. It was an old-fashioned tram, open sided and with wooden seats. It was essentially a cart that was completely open to the elements. I had evidently been noticed as absent. My father was away so the rest of family spread out and commenced the search. My uncle was driving on the main street when he saw the tram. He then saw me on one of the wooden seats. He stopped the tram and took me home. Thank goodness the train had open sides and I was fortuitously seen. To this day I have no idea how I got on the tram, or what the tram driver was thinking about this apparently motherless child.

## ◼ PRIMARY SCHOOL

From the age of five, I started Primary School but I started with the advantage of having been taught to read and write by my mother. The reading and writing skill made me a mad reader and I have since always had three or four books on the go. The school was run by two sisters who were lovely women. Aside from the reading I remember there were egg and spoon races. I was quite fast, probably pre-trained from all the running away from everyone. By six or seven I was being entered into races.

## ◼ PREPARATORY SCHOOL

Preparatory school took me from seven to nine years of age. It was where I had my first taste of acting. I was cast in the nativity play. A blue-eyed English boy on whom I had a massive crush was cast as Joseph but every time we had to be close to each other to rehearse, I fainted. I was obviously besotted. Rehearsing became impossible so what did the teachers do? They recast Joseph as an older girl, and I no longer fainted. There were also another two young neighbourhood boys that I fancied. Clearly my 'mad for boys' thing had begun and had started early.

It was at this school when I was asked what I wanted to be when I grew up. I replied, 'actress'. I don't think it was as a result of my nativity play experience. I can only think that I must have seen movie magazines somewhere that gave me the idea of being an 'actress'. As there was no TV at all in Jamaica at the time, I did not even get to watch TV until I was 13 years old and in London.

## ■ HIGHSCHOOL (BIG SCHOOL)

From nine, I went to High School. By now, this was the time when we were living in the house that my grandfather had made for my mother. We were back at Drominagh, but in a new and different house. Both Preparatory and High School were private schools. It was in High School where I met my best friend, Betty Holtz. We started school on the same day and she became a big part of my life, my 'bestest' friend. We were considered to be two of the prettiest girls in the school and we were both gorgeous in our little 10-year-old bodies. I'm not sure we were sprouting by then but we were both boys mad. We would have sleep overs at each other's houses.

We decided we needed to practice kissing on each other. We wanted to make sure that when we met our boys, we were really good. The first time we tried, we were disgusted with putting our tongues in each other's mouths; it was revolting. But then, we started to quite like it. We continued the trial runs. It was our little foray into lesbianism, or girl power. It became our naughty little secret. We became fabulous kissers, and we could not wait to demonstrate to the boys how good we were. They were not disappointed.

My first kiss was a foray into seduction. A handsome teenage boy who passed my gate every day was my target. I had been watching him for a while. I came home from school and I put on my tiny shorts and skimpiest top. Then I climbed up on a gate post and sat waiting for him. He arrived. I whistled at him and, surprised and curious, he stopped. I opened the gate and invited him in with an offer of a glass of water. Then sitting together, I somehow encouraged him to kiss me, after which, he hurried off in fear of getting caught. I was 11 or 12, he was 14 or 15. The wild child has had her sexual awakening! I was also sprouting and had begun my period. This horrified me as I had not been informed and I guiltily thought I had done damage to myself due to my secret bathroom activities. Discarded knickers were discovered and I was given 'the talk'. I was feeling quite womanly at this turn of events.

Both Betty and I were athletes, sprinters, high jumpers, netball and tennis players. We were top in our class at school. We were sporting rivals but because we loved each other so much it did not become a problem. Although we were equally athletic, she was better at ballet. I was too large for that form of dance, and I had bigger feet.

I was good at languages, specifically Latin, good at art, essays, literature, and geography. History was beyond boring; I had a boring teacher. And I was dreadful at maths. However, when the reports came through, a note said, 'Martine does not apply herself sufficiently, and she is a perpetual dreamer.'

I was maid of honour at Betty's wedding. I remember seeing her 20 years later in Florida when we had a date to see each other. The occasion was marked by an incredible thunderstorm and lightening. She was dressed in white; I was in black, 'This is really dramatic,' we agreed, 'But don't mention our lesbian thing.' She was a fabulous woman; unfortunately, we lost touch.

I was eight years old when my parents divorced and, in a way, I was not surprised. It was the 1940s, there was a lack of jobs as a Busha. He had gone to America a few times to work whereby he was gone for several months at a time. He returned and we were all together living in the Crossroads rental place. I heard my father say, 'We should have more children' But my mother said, 'No Ronnie, no way.' I can see why she would not want any more children with him being away so often and for so long. Then he went to the Dominican Republic; this was the final nail in their relationship. He went to be the Busha of a banana plantation and he fell in love with a lovely young Spanish woman. He fell for a woman who was the daughter of the owners of the plantation he was working for.

Daddy later married the woman and had five children with her.

I missed my Daddy; I was his girl. I did wonder in my child brain how my parents had ever stayed together for so long as they were so completely different. I saw him again when I came back from England to Jamaica before my 18th birthday. Along with my Beswick grandmother, Amy, we took a boat to visit Daddy and his wife, who by then was on her third child. We spent a month in the Dominican Republic. I saw him again in my 30s in the Dominican Republic as part of a 'roots trip'. They had by then five children. Daddy never left the Dominican Republic. I really loved his wife; her name was Amantina. She was only a little older than me; she was much younger than my father. I could see their relationship and I saw how much she loved and cared for him.

That was the last time I ever saw him.

Mummy was sad for a while but my beloved grandfather, my mother's father, came to the rescue when he gave her the piece of Drominagh land on which he built her the house.

My aunt Veva, the comedian of the family, and Uncle Rudolph, parents to my three cousins, Michael, Donny and Patrick, set up a projector and a screen in the back yard of the house under the mango trees. Benches were set up for all the aunts, uncles and cousins. I loved Laurel and Hardy. It was here where we also put on our little home grown shows and comedies. Much raucous laughter ensued. We were allowed to be common then.

## ■ GRANDFATHER

George Norman Penso was an extraordinary man who commanded a great deal of respect and love from all his family and extended family. He was Big Daddy to seven children; four girls and three boys. As was the norm in many Jamaican families, the mix of race and colour was very apparent; the colours ranged from black to white.

Grandfather owned different and varied businesses. He owned a fabric store in downtown Kingston which prompted him to travel the world in search of fabrics. He also owned two gas stations; one in Crossroads and one in Kingston. He was known as a coach builder of horse drawn carriages. He owned one and would take the grandchildren, two at a time, on little jaunts around the property. I have no idea how he acquired all these businesses but he evidently was a good business man. He had all the businesses by the time I knew him. His whole family worked in his businesses. The eldest daughter ran a gas station, the eldest son ran the other gas station and my mummy worked at the fabric store. I remember there was something quite magical about touching and feeling the fabric. I got to be a little sales woman to the regular customers, "We have a new fabric, you might like this."

My grandfather's mode of transport was a stunning 1940s American Oldsmobile; a prized possession in jet black with an abundance of shiny chrome that we all admired. We believe he bought it from Kingston, or perhaps it was imported. It was just gorgeous, a stunning car with huge amounts of chrome. It was so exciting to ride in it and it was an amazing sight to see on the roads as you really didn't see a lot of those cars in Jamaica. As he got older, mummy became his driver. I saw the car again when I returned to Jamaica in 1961 but thereafter, I know not what happened to it.

One of his ways of relaxing was to take afternoon naps in a hammock. He had two hammocks. One was at the fabric store and one was at his Drominagh home. In the store, he had a space which was part store room, part office. He had the hammock permanently placed and set up in this room. He had his lunch delivered to him in these amazing stacked trays like the Indian dabbawalas, and after lunch he would have a nap for a half an hour. His home hammock was in the veranda and was only hung up when needed, and taken down when not used. It was his weekend hammock, again for after lunch. Sometimes I would climb in and take a nap with him. I still have a memory of the scent on him, he smoked cigars. I love hammocks so much that, when I moved to England, I set one up in my garden in London under my banana trees! And when I moved to my next place, it would come with me.

He also had a favourite rocking chair where he would partake of a glass of brandy with his cigar; also on the veranda, this sat on the opposite side to the hammock. It was a green cane rocking chair, high backed, lovely, and perfect for his cigar and brandy. He played Chinese Checkers with his sister while he rocked. And now, so too do I love playing this game.

There was a Grand Piano in the house. Sometimes he would say to me "Play for me, Roses" (his name for me) and I would run to the Grand Piano and throw my hands across the keys, composing my own symphonies as I played. I loved this piano. I didn't know what I was doing and I couldn't reach the pedals. But when I could reach the pedals, well then, there was no stopping me. To this day, "Roses" still performs concertos to the disbelief of friends who know that I have never had a lesson and I cannot read music. I still have a piano in my home. My film composer friend, Peter Robinson, who was a brilliant pianist, heard one of Roses' compositions, and was sweetly complimentary. He told me about a Russian woman who apparently did exactly the same thing as I do. However, she had recorded her compositions. Perhaps I should consider my next career…

Every Sunday afternoon at Drominagh was always an absolute delight. The whole extended family gathered for Aunt Zelia's tea and delicious cakes and cookies. She also made a fabulous ice cream which was churned by hand in a huge bucket by one of the servants. There were numerous gatherings for Easter, Christmas and birthdays. And when we were at Albion, we would have picnics on the private beach and feasts in the Great House.

Whenever he felt like it, my grandfather organised our outings. And, once it was decided, they happened quickly. The food, the family, the servants, all had to be ready. It was always thrilling. We would travel in the Oldsmobile, and everyone else in their cars. Another special outing was a trip to the Rockfort Mineral Baths; a spa for massages and mineral baths. There were two private swimming pools and several individual baths that could be hired for brief periods of time. He would hire one of the two main baths for the family. A bizarre thing to think he would hire it like this. This was the 1940s. But again, the whole family would pile into cars and off we would go for our mineral baths.

Aunt Zelia was his third wife and adored by all. Although she was our step grandmother, for some reason she was always known as Aunt Zelia. She was the garden expert; she had and maintained a beautiful flower garden which was her pride and joy. There was a team of servants who cared for the livestock, and cooked and cleaned for the family. They were all housed in separate buildings on the property. There were cows that gave milk early in the morning, there were horses for the buggy, there was livestock for the meats, there were pigeons kept in the aviary. These last invariably became soup. My grandfather loved pigeon soup. The pigeons were his favourite animals. And together with becoming soup, they taught us all about sex. Jamaican pigeons; they are always at it. There was so much sex going on between these birds, which was just as well as they were eaten as fast as they reproduced. Actually, we learnt about sex from all the animals. When I was about eight years old, I questioned in the religiously focused Sunday School how come Mary had had a baby by herself when all the animals had to 'do it' to produce babies. As this created total confusion with the other children, I was immediately removed from Sunday School.

I am so lucky and privileged to have grown up in such an incredible family and I do hold my grandfather entirely responsible for my caviar taste in life. I think we always knew we were privileged. Family names was basically how class was judged. The Penso family was held in high regard. So, we were aware from an early age.

———————

I remember I woke up one morning in Jamaica and had a major realisation that my capacity for love had no bounds, either for people or for places. My Island Jamaica still makes my heart sing when I think of how beautiful it is. So many of my memories are almost tangible. The smell of the earth after a tropical rainfall

27

and the glorious sunsets. The heat and the soft breezes that relieves the sting. The amazing variety of trees with flowers and fruit. Driving on a country road and stopping for a coconut water being sold out of an old fridge on wheels. The ingenuity of the people and their wonderful sense of humour. The incredible north coast beaches with their white sand and warm aquamarine waters which have their own unique smells. The rivers and waterfalls and the lush green mountains. All are beloved memories. But we were shortly to be leaving Jamaica.

# 5

## 1954-1959

# ENGLAND, TEENAGE

---

It is fair to say my sister and I were considered to be the princesses of our family. Every day, we had to be dressed and ready to meet Mummy and the family when they returned from work after 4pm. We had always to sit elegantly with our knees together. Personally, I could not wait to spread my legs and sit more comfortably. And where in the world is this polite behaviour best exemplified but in England. My mother was attached to the mother country; she positively revered it. And so, she thought it would be perfect to take her princesses to be educated in London.

Before we left Jamaica, we had no idea how it was going to work out. Mummy had a friend who worked at the Home Office in England and whom we would meet upon landing. In terms of the preparation required before leaving the heat of the tropics, my mother made coats for us all and double lined them for warmth. In fact, she made all our heavier clothes with the fabrics from my grandfather's shop. In the end though, we were still not prepared enough for the cold of England.

We took a banana boat. The 70-80 passengers boarded in Kingston and then we headed to Port Antonio where they loaded the bananas for the trans-Atlantic voyage. I remember seeing the long procession of people all with the bananas piled on their heads, all walking in single file and into the hold where the bananas were stored. It was an amazing sight, the only thing missing was the singing of the banana song. The boat was lovely; it was actually a boat that was designed to ferry both goods and passengers. I was 12, my sister was 10; we were the only young girls on the boat and we had the complete freedom to explore and play.

Mary Rose and Laurellie Ann and cousin

Mummy takes her two princesses to England

We played with the dogs that were being shipped to London, we played with the workers, we played with everyone. We were still the little princesses. It was a very exciting two weeks.

We landed in Southampton. Dorothy, mummy's friend from Home Office, met us. She was very very English. I remember thinking she had English legs, which is to say her ankles were not fine. Not fat, not skinny, just, English. I was such a princess. We were shown to a boarding house in Regent's Park. It was one big room with a big bed. It was so cold, we all three of us got in together. We were not there for long. We went to live in Wimbledon for a short while. We attended the local school but something was off. It might have been some experience to do with racism as I was white and my sister was brown. People did not know Jamaicans or about the heritage that can create within a single family, children of different colours. We did not stay there long either.

We moved to Kingston and into a lovely flat by the river owned by an Indian family. The property had three flats. There was a South African family in one flat, the Indian owners in another, and us. There was a young son in the South African family called Martin. He was seven years old and he called me his Marylyn Monroe. We were all friends; everyone was friendly and on occasion we would all watch TV with them. My lovely little Martin would climb on my lap and cuddle with me. While I allowed it because he was lovely, the cuddles got a little fresh from time to time and he was so in love that he decided he was going to kiss me. And he gave me a proper kiss; it knocked me back as I was twice his age. As a matter of fact, every now and again I still hear from him.

We would take long walks by the river. I went to Tolworth Grammar School but we found that the education level there was not as good as that which I had experienced in the Jamaican private schools.

Mummy didn't have to work as my grandfather was helping us a lot. Maybe the house we left behind had been sold, or maybe it was being rented out to provide for my mother's income. Grandfather was always supporting us in his generous ways. That said, mummy did find a job for a brief moment at a department store called Bentalls.

The Indian family had bought themselves a bus to go travelling. As they were giving up the house, everyone had to move out. Mummy found the best flat on Kew Green at 10 guineas a week. Today, the house would rent for easily £4000/

month. Two bedrooms, a bay window, a garden; it was a fabulous house that became our home for the last three years of our time in London.

We had house parties. We hooked up with a skiffle musicians' group who played traditional jazz. With much laughter and flirting, we became great friends. Mummy was clever; she allowed them to come to the house to rehearse so she could keep an eye on us and the flirting. I was mad for one of the musicians, a banjo player, but nothing happened; I was still too young, and I wasn't giving it out yet. I liked the kissing. We kissed a lot, but nothing else. I was 15…! I even sang with them on one occasion in a performance, not just a rehearsal; I sang *Summer Time*.

There was a place called Eel Pie Island which was quite well-known for entry level jazz musicians. The music was fabulous. We all went there to dance; it had a dance floor that bounced and encouraged mad dancing. It had a reputation for a lot of hanky panky. At the time I was going there, to get on to the Island you had to take a boat. It was also forbidden to me because of that aforementioned reputation. But of course, I ignored that and managed to go there quite often. That would equate to be about a couple of times a month, but I had to be careful for my mother not to suspect my rule-breaking.

This period of time saw the start of my rebellion. I decided I didn't want to be in school. I had discovered Richmond and it was to become my playground. I discovered and became friends with a bunch of bohemians. There was a very famous coffee shop opposite Richmond Bridge called L'Auberge. We would sit together discussing Lord knows what while consuming loads of coffee and smoking loads of cigarettes. I wanted to do it more often and I did not want to go to school, so I played truant on many a day. My mother would watch me get on a bus to Ealing, and then I got off and went the other way.

I had a friend at Tolworth who left that school to go full time to a drama school. It was a school that taught you everything that you learn at a normal school but with a heavy slant towards drama that included Acting, Dancing and Performing. It was run by Nora Webber who would later go on to greater things. She also offered in the same school additional classes for people who attended other schools.

I got to be in this school for a while, and I performed at Richmond Theatre. It was a truly wonderful experience. I played a native American Indian and wore the full Indian costume that my mother had made for me. It was all children. I didn't have any lines; it was all mime. I was miming the stroking of non-existent animals.

There was one little problem; upon bending over, my trousers split and to my great embarrassment, I had to slowly back out of the stage.

My sister had begun to pick up some seriously non-princess like behaviour. Her speech had become terrible, very low class, and utterly awful. Mummy was horrified. She moved her into a private girls' school in Surbiton that made their pupils wear a purple uniform. All of which was very expensive, so mummy decided I did not need to go to Acting school. There was a big fight which led to the forming of an agreement whereby if I agreed to having a career back-up and learn typing, book-keeping, and secretarial skills, then she would send me to Pitmans College and then later, maybe, she would support my desire to attend drama schools. Now, this worked because Pitmans was a co-educational college; there were boys to flirt with, and also a drama teacher for my acting. I started and stayed for two years.

I was 16 and it was time to get a job. I left Pitmans and found a job at the Institute of Patentees and Inventors in the Victoria area of London. There was the Office President/Manager, Mr Sutherland, and a secretary. I became the junior secretary. On the Board of the Institute were the CEOs of big companies who once a month came into the office for meetings, cigar smoking and drinking. In my youth, they were all old; in their 50s and 60s. I would take the minutes of the meetings. I was not very good at short hand, and if that wasn't enough, I would also fall asleep. He would call me, 'Mary, did you get that?' 'I seemed to have missed out on some things.' I would reply. And he would help me fill in the blanks.

All the inventors came in with utterly wild inventions, and I would get the patents for them. I would go through the particulars, and I would visit a patent office to request the patent, and attend meetings with the inventors. I remember one particular invention which this woman had created. It was a typewriter that typed musical notes. This was absolutely amazing; I was fascinated. Unfortunately, I left England before anything could happen to progress this invention. This part of the job, I was good at and so I became the publicity girl. I started at £7 per week. As I was good with people, three months later I got a raise to £7 10 shillings per week. This was fun. The inventions were amazing and I presented them to the CEOs to discuss their progression. It was a really groovy place.

There was one occasion when Mr Sutherland tried to get fresh with me. He was a big man, slightly on the fat side, but you don't get fresh with me without consequences. There was a copy machine called the Gestetner where you put ink in and turn a lever to produce copies. I was making copies when he came up behind me and a little close to me. Maybe he was looking for a hug. 'If you do that again, I am going to squeeze this ink all over you.' He didn't do that again.

There were various boyfriends, but I was still not ready for that just yet. I came across the boys at the Saint Paul Public School. They were bad boys; I liked them but I had to swipe their hands away when they got fresh. I was 14 when I had my first proper boyfriend, and whereby my mother offered her approval. 'Yes, you can have this one.' He was 19 and called Peter. My girlfriends and I were hanging out at a school fence watching these workers, these young men working with their shirts off. This made us all very giggly and I decided to whistle at them. At which point one of them came over and started to talk to me. What have I done? I thought. Now what. He was gorgeous and very respectful, and asked for a date. How excited was I! He came to the flat and talked to my mother. She agreed to allow me to take a walk with him. We went to the river and of course there was kissing involved; my favourite thing. He was going into the army as part of the National Service so our little affaire-ette was short but sweet. A few weeks, a little walk, a little kiss. He did write me lovely letters when he went away. The song I remember at that time was Elvis Presley's Heartbreak Hotel.

I started to explore my caviar tastes in London as handed down to me by my grandfather. I used to go off and have lunch by myself in a lovely restaurant in Ealing. I would have a three-course meal. I later joined a church group who put on operettas and allowed me to explore the acting; this was fun.
But at this point, my sister had turned herself around and had become first class. By comparison, I was now the common one. She was the goody, I was not; I was a bit out of control. I was 17 when in 1959, Mummy decided she was missing her family and that we were returning to Jamaica.

I have enormous respect for my mother to rip our family apart as she did for our benefit. We were very tight knit and close family. Many years later, she said that perhaps it was probably not a very good idea to have taken us there. And I said, 'Absolutely not. It was the best thing you ever did for us Mummy.'

# 6

## 1959-1961

# JAMAICA, REBELLION

---

We returned to Jamaica by a Norwegian ship. I'm not sure how we found it, but again, Mummy did everything. It was a small ship called the North Star. It wasn't a cargo or cruise ship, just a passenger ship this time. It was probably decided upon, because it was the right price. It again took two weeks and it was really lovely. My sister and I were now teenagers, and again we really had the run of the ship. In fact, we were the only two teenagers as passengers. Still, we were the Princesses. As a family, we were treated to sit at the captain's table for dinner. Again, I have no idea how or why. Perhaps it was because we found ourselves amongst all the officers, maybe because Mummy was very attractive; I'm not sure. The feeling I have is that once we had forged a friendship, we were sitting at his dining table with the officers all the time.

Both Mummy and I had little stories with the crew. Mummy flirted with the 2nd Officer. Every evening there was dancing. And whenever there was dancing, Mummy danced. She liked her dance. So, it probably began with a dance, and then a stroll, and I think actually it went a little further.

I met and flirted with a young engineer officer called Bernt. He was rather gorgeous, quite tall, with green eyes, really lovely. Of course, the fact that they all wore their lovely white uniforms in the evening did not hinder the attraction. He was in his mid to late 20s. I fancied him, and obviously he thought I was fanciable. There was a lot of flirting. It became quite serious, and I made the decision.

I chose him to be my first lover. I think later in life I realised that when we decided to give it up, it was us girls that made the decision. And so, he was the one. He was kind, he was lovely; and of course, he was on a boat which travelled back and forth between places, so our little romance couldn't and wasn't to be regular or long-term thing. This thinking opened the door to later follies.

After our journey home, both Mummy and I arranged to see them again. They made a return trip from Norway to Jamaica. We had a date to go to our favourite nightclub called the Glass Bucket in Kingston, Saint Andrew, near Half Way Tree, and we had a lovely evening. We danced, we drank, but we all realised it wasn't going to work and so of course, we drifted apart and lost touch. Mummy and I didn't really discuss any of our adventures after that; perhaps had they been wearing their uniforms on our date it might have all lasted a little longer…

We arrived in Jamaica and we stayed at Drominagh, but not at Mummy's house that my grandfather had built for her. We stayed in the Great House. I have no idea what happened to Mummy's house since we had first left for England; perhaps it had been sold.

And so, the prodigals had returned. There was a big welcome that was something like the Sunday afternoon gatherings and big feasts as had been arranged by my grandfather. Grandfather was delighted to see us all again. And he was back in his element whereby he could just take good care of us.

We stayed at Drominagh for a month before we rented our first house in Stony Hill. We were in the hills now, the foothills above St Andrew; a very rich and well-to-do area. My mother had a car now.

I began to work for BWIA (British West Indian Airways) as the junior secretary to the Manager. I think I found the job through word of mouth and the family name that sort of just suggested I would be right for the job without even undertaking an interview. I had also just returned from the aspirationally sounding England which offered a promise to the securing of this or any job. BWIA had offices all over the islands. I ditch shorthand and become efficient in typing from a Dictaphone. It was a big deal to be in this office. Even as a junior secretary, I was an assistant to the top secretary. But I was soon in trouble again. In trying to take minutes of the meetings, I missed some of the details; I really was not very good at it. The book keeping and anything that involved a Dictaphone, I was good at that. In the end, it all turned out nicely as the ex-ballet teacher secretary for whom

I worked was kind and she covered for me.

All the top assistant managers were much older than me. They all looked after different departments and they were all married. I was transferred to one of the managers and began an affair with him. He was the manager of the Publicity department. He was quite lovely, very good looking, very funny, quick witted, around 30, and it was just him and me in the office. He would brush my arm, little moments, tactile. He was married with children. I knew that. I kind of fell in love, or lust, with him. It continued on and off for a while, less than a year, until he got transferred to another island like Trinidad or Barbados.

Regularly, at the end of the working day around 4.00pm, I would meet up with a gang of men for drinks. It was similar to the office whereby I liked hanging out with the fellas. The afternoon gang were all drinkers of rum. There were maybe a couple of other girls that would join us and every afternoon, we would meet at the Jamaica Inn, or another bar, and drink all night. It was getting worse. I had basically become an alcoholic and pill popper. Uppers were available over the counter and were in regular use by us all. And when I wasn't with the week day gang, I had a whole other weekend gang that I danced all night with at the Glass Bucket. I was enjoying myself. Too much.

I was at the office for the full two years. And the fun continued apace for the same duration. I had a moment when I realised that actually, I was really angry at having left my beloved London. I was too young to have been allowed to have remained by myself and I began to understand that this behaviour was a reactive rebellion to being forced to leave London. I was destroying my life. I was still able to function through the days, but it was to get worse.

## ■ MODELLING

There were many modelling shows in Kingston for department stores, or designers, or hotels that had clothes stores. They were held in either hotels or nightclubs and the presentation was like that of a show; it presented an evening's entertainment. As part of the entertainment, there would also be a dance show, or a singer, but we were all a part of that 'show'. My friends and I were considered to be the best-looking girls in town and we were all up for this. We became the showgirls.

Along with my friend Betty and other girlfriends, I became one of the main models where they would say, 'Betty and Mary, we will have them.' We all worked elsewhere during the day; in banks, airlines and stores. And we were also from well-known families; they knew who we were. I ended up in doing this on and off for two years and it gave me enough exposure to be entered in to the Miss Jamaica competition.

The girls, the competitors, were chosen by the sponsors and the company people who attended the fashion shows. They saw the models and they would choose who entered the Miss Jamaica contest. I was Miss Whirlpool (Fridges, Freezers) and it was a banner by that name that I would have to wear for the duration of the competition. I had to wear it across the fabulous gown, or the skimpy swim suit. However, on the day of the competition, I was still drunk from the night before and I obliterated any chance of my winning. This was the only time I ever competed in Miss Jamaica. The information online informs that I was Miss Jamaica, but no, I never won.

The modelling also led me to doing three or four tourist board films. My favourite such film showed me leisurely going down the Rio Grande on a bamboo raft from Port Antonio. There were two of us including the guide. We headed down the rapids, we swam, we behaved like tourists, and we got paid. Another film had me advertising the Awarak Hotel near Dunn's River Falls. I would be there in my bikini lying by the pool, relaxing, enjoying myself and inspiring the tourists with a look that said, 'I am having such fun, you will too!' I loved doing these films; they were fun and we went to all the best places.

I continued having the extra marital affairs. I was on a self-destructive course and my poor Mother was at her wits end. I never had affairs with my weekend dancing boys. They were my age and just as bad with the ladies. The dancers and the drinkers, they were my weekend fun. I chose, or preferred, older men who were all married. They never ended well. One ending was very horrible, because his wife had found out and she confronted me. It was very embarrassing. The affairs were lustful, but the drunken idiot within me also thought I was in love.

One morning I arrived home at 6am having not slept or eaten for weeks. Our loved and trusted maid found me on the kitchen floor, shaking uncontrollably. My normal pattern had been to come home when the sun was up, usually around 4-5am. I would have a shower; I was usually picked up by another worker and I would be at work for 8am. But that morning, the pattern incontrovertibly broke. I could not continue to pull it together forever as a lack of sleep or food would inevitably find my limits. I called my mother; my mother called the doctor and I was immediately admitted to hospital where I was put on a sleep cure for 10 days. I was put to sleep, the doctors hooked me up and they fed me intravenously. It would take the full 10 days to bring me back to a form of balance. Incredibly, during all this time my job was kept open for me.

This was a serious wakeup call and I heard it. I was shocked that I had to be put into hospital and that I had got to this point. It was really shocking. When I came out, I realised that I had to pull myself together, and that I needed to get back to London. But that would cost money and of course, I had been spending all my money. I knew I had to do something. This whole period was marked as a form of rebellion by my having to be in Jamaica. Jamaica was too small for me; everyone knew everyone's business. It was not where I wanted to be. There was always this desire to go back to London. While there had been, if not a plan, then a hope, I had been going the other way, 'I'll show you who I am.' But it was a way filled with self-harm and self-destruction. I stayed off the drink and I ate properly. It didn't stop me from later going back to it all, but it was never in the same way as it had been for the last two years. A control button had been installed; my head had been turned around.

I saw a beauty competition advertised. It was to be put on by a huge automobile sales place in Kingston called Autoville. The winner would thus be crowned Miss Autoville. I had never worked with or for them before. Putting on a beauty pageant meant for them publicity. Modelling was a big part of life in Jamaica, it was always there, people always wanted us, the models, to be around. So, people put on competitions; they would have clothes designed for us, and we were feted. In the case of Miss Autoville, the prize was a brand-new Morris Minor. All the girlfriends entered. I realised this was my chance so, by myself, I flew up to Montego Bay on the north coast for some isolated preparation. Luckily the job gave me good access to cheap flights. I booked myself into a beach hotel and I slept, rested, ate and sunned myself. No drinking. The sand was white and the beaches were lovely. I was determined to win.

I flew back down to Kingston. The competition took place over a long weekend; something like Friday to Sunday. There were 20 girls. We had to make appearances at three venues; a racetrack, a hotel, and then a big night somewhere at another hotel. I really enjoyed myself and, I won! I received the crown and the car. It was a soft top, red and cream. However, on examining the car, my mother and her brother discovered that it was not a new car but in fact a second-hand example! Mummy and my uncle confronted the owner and demanded the compensation or they would expose the deceit. The owner never stood a chance. When they were determined, it was the dragon lady and the dragon man. I received the compensation; money.

This was the ticket to my freedom. Along with Laurellie and Mummy and four of my best friends who had been influenced and inspired by my tales of London, I booked my flight to London. Mummy finally realised I had to go; it had painfully occurred to her that I was not very happy in Jamaica. It was time to go. Coincidentally, my sister wanted to be a nurse and was of an age to study. Mummy thought it might be the perfect time to happen; it all tied in. We all left for London.

# 7

# LONDON, MY DREAM AS AN ACTRESS

I arrived in London with my four girlfriends. We were all aged between 16 and 19 and, perhaps due to feeling responsible for encouraging them to come to London, I became the den mother. I found a flat in Whitton near Twickenham to suit us all and, after signing the lease, I installed everyone. Actually, I do not know how I managed to do all that. I then contacted some of my Bohemian friends in Richmond, who all lived in a shared house.

I had a bit of money to tide me over but all of us in the flat found work as temporary secretaries. Secretarial work was the easy back up and through temping agencies, we could work immediately. We would go to the agency, they would find a job for which they thought we would be suitable, and then the agency would take us on VW bus to the company. We might be there for a day, a week, a bit longer. The agency would have all the details on paper of what the companies needed but as we didn't have phones, we would get to the agency and just wait until something became available. I worked this way on and off for a few months. Eventually, I would get into a company where I would then stay for much longer; upwards of three months. In the meantime, I also found a way to model. Again, I have no recollection as to how I found this.

In the evenings and weekends, we hung out at the house of my Bohemian friends. They grew marijuana in window boxes so I was introduced to the delights of a spliff. They were four guys, beatniks, a bit older than us, a bit criminal; they

42

had been in a bit of trouble, but they got away with marijuana. They were our protectors, they were fun. There was lots of flirting. We held my 20th birthday at their house. It was a wild toga or bed sheets party. It was filled with much fun, laughter and dancing. We were stoned and drunk, it really was the best time. And then of course, the bed sheets started to fall off. Mad teenagers.

The flat in Whitton lasted only for six months. While it was a brand new flat, the property had a ghost. Everyone had ghostly experiences; we told each other our stories and we fled the place. We later discovered a couple who had been living there had been electrocuted. While we were living there, the lights would turn on and off and the stove would switch on and off. Prior to our leasing the flat, it had been empty for some time. Of course.

My best friend, Esther Anderson, split from the shared living group and found a flat close to the river in Chelsea on Blantyre Street. My sister, Laurellie, was in Kingston Hospital studying to be a nurse and would come to us when she had a day off to tell us stories of working with dead people.

Both Esther and I were doing office work, however I discovered a way into modelling by joining an Agency that had a training school and which led to in-house modelling. This was where you were hired at a daily rate of 10 guineas for a period of a month to show the 'house' clothes to buyers. Fashion houses would have a line of clothes which they would sell only to buyers. There might be several different lines in the collection. These houses were not high-end designers; they made clothes for what would suit general stores. When modelling the clothes, many different designers and buyers would collect at the venue or salon for the show. Everyone was smoking madly at the time. We were very good at being flirty and fun; it amused them, and we sold the clothes.

There were two other models who became my dear friends and we would all be hired together every year by the same house. We were a bright fun trio and the clients adored us. Marilyn the bubbly blonde, Alex the tall red head with a great sense of humour, and me the flirty brunette. The fashion shows were held in two of the four seasons, Spring and Autumn. We were also doing photo shoots so we were able to pay our respective rents and bills. We were all dancers, and this was the time of the discotheque, or clubs. Our first disco was Les Ambassadeurs and every time a new club opened, we would be there. We would put on impromptu shows where we would dance together to our favourite songs such as *Da Do Ron Ron* by The Crystals; everyone loved this one.

43

While Esther and I were in Jamaica, Esther had been having an affair with a married man and I too was with another married man. The men were each other's best friends. Mine was called Biggie, hers Gilly. They even looked alike; both were dark, handsome and had green eyes. We fled all that, but we did have this in common. While in London, Esther met Chris Blackwell, the owner of Island Records and later owner of Ian Fleming's Jamaican home called Goldeneye. Both Jamaican, she began having an affair with him. We gave up the Chelsea flat and moved in with him at Connaught Square. Coming from a very wealthy family, he had rented this huge house with four or five floors which he filled by renting rooms to his Jamaican friends. It is the way Chris does things. Winston Stona, a Jamaican actor, was in the top floor room. Francine Winham, a rebellious debutante, was Winston's girlfriend. Francine's father owned half of Mayfair; she came from a very wealthy family. She was a bohemian and she liked her Jamaican men. Sally Densham, Chris's ex-girlfriend, lived on the next floor. Known as Sally D, she was a top window dresser at Selfridges. She had several Australian girlfriends who used to visit; Evelyn, Gail and Norma who all became my true sisters. Esther and Chris lived in the master bedroom and I lived on the same floor. In the basement lived Jackie Edwards, a very talented Ska singer and song writer. So, there was a lot of Ska music in the house. The tenants really became a family. We had one large fridge where we put our names on everything. But of course, there was stealing. 'Who took the last of my milk? And where's my bloody cheddar?' would often be heard yelled through the house. And so, I retaliated and stole too. It was just one of the funniest times.

Chris had started Island Records and he had come to London to widen its exposure. I had met him briefly in Jamaica, but in London was where I really got to know him. Chris and Esther were great together. She was a spitfire. He enjoyed winding her up and they would go at it with each other to then all end in laughter. Chris' first hit was *My Boy Lollipop* by Millie Small, this adorable little 15-year-old girl who later became a superstar. Esther and Francine took care of her.

Francine and Esther worked with Chris on Island Records in England. They packed the records in his minivan and delivered them to all the Jamaican stores in Brixton and other slightly seedy areas of the UK. I think he really loved doing the rounds. Chris predominantly promoted Ska music but he also promoted risqué comedy albums such as Music to Strip By. Hilarious. We were brought in to sew G Strings and to put them on the album covers. What he was doing? I have no idea, but we all joined in.

I brought my drums from Jamaica. Winston would play my drums, to which I would do my creative dancing. Francine would play the grand piano and we would sing together. Our favourite song to sing to was the Everly Brothers song, *Bye Bye Love*, which we thought could get us started as singers! Francine continued singing opera and blues up until her death a few years ago. She was very rich and she could do anything. She would hire places and perform concerts; I would always go to see her. She was one of my dearest friends and I later spent wonderful times at her country house 'Joldwynds' in Surrey; a beautiful historic art deco house that looks like a big boat. It was one of those houses that are always being rented out for TV and film shows. She was the most brilliant and generous hostess.

I was by now doing much more modelling and had stopped doing the secretarial work. It was here from where came the beginnings of my film work. Models were also being hired as extras to pretty things up on screen and I did some of this too. I did not work through an Extra agency; it would be the modelling agency that would send me. It was very definitely the way to go to get a foot in the acting door. From time to time, you would also be given a line and it was at this point that I considered taking acting classes. In this capacity I did an episode of *Danger Man* with Patrick McGoohan and some other TV series.

### 1962

While in Jamaica, a very nice film producer, Robert Schultz, arrived looking for a star in the making. He met several girls and I was chosen as his protégé. He took me to Montego Bay, put me up in a hotel and filmed me on the beach, playing, being. I just happened to have a yellow polka dot bikini – it was at the same time as the hot pop song of the same name.

He was a lovely guy and a perfect gentleman. How lucky was I to have a producer who did not in any way come on to me. He took the film to London and showed it to MCA. A month later, I received a letter from them saying 'If I was ever in London, I should come in to see them.'

I had no idea what MCA was and I had no idea about agencies. I was totally green about the world of acting agencies and so it took me a while before I called them. They gave me an appointment for an interview. I went into the room and there were 10 suits sitting there, looking me up and down. I was 20 and I was thinking, 'What's this, what is this, who are all these men?' Then I heard the name James Bond. I hadn't heard of the name or the character before but they decided to set up an interview with the director for the role of Honeychile Ryder, the lead female role for *Dr No*. The director turned out to be Terence Young. It was a brief audition, as he quickly realised that I had no experience. We had a connection though. He said, 'You are too young, you have no experience. Go and get some and then we can discuss an idea I have for you.' I liked him, I heard him and I did exactly what he said.

Terence was lovely and was true to his word. I feel lucky to have had someone who did what they said they would, and did not try to jump on me. So, I started getting some experience and I joined an acting class. I took a class with a teacher who was really a creepy little guy who tried to jump on me. And of course I was not having that. I didn't stay very long. My modelling agency would get requests for their models to appear in various TV episodes and series to provide beauty and glamour. Sometimes you would get that one line and this became the beginning of my acting career. I did two or three things. One was a comedy where I played this island girl in a very funny sitcom. By the time I saw Terence again, it was socially and through Chris Blackwell. Terence and Chris had become friends. The connection between Terence and I continued. I didn't see him very often, but enough to see that our connection had not and would never change. He had a mischievous smile all the time, and I loved him for it. He was the greatest gentleman I ever knew. He looked after us, he loved champagne, and we became friends. I was spoiled by being introduced to Terence and thereby the film industry because I never had to lose my knickers for any bloody producers. He made me a promise, and he kept it.

I was hanging out with other groups of people now. Robert Hartford-Davies was a director of kitchen sink dramas. I met him and he introduced me to his group of actors. I was then hired to do a music video for Craig Douglas; a singer not of my taste but he was hot at the time. It was for a song called *Town Crier* and the video started with a town crier. I was the town crier wearing a little short outfit, high heels and stockings.

Robert's next film was *Saturday Night Out* where he cast me as a bar tender, 'Time gentleman please.' It was his first major film and it had a good cast that included Heather Sears, Bernard Lee and Margaret Nolan. It was the time of the kitchen sink dramas. It was filmed in black and white and was a bit dark. It was not a huge film but it was a good film. I was very excited, but I also felt at ease because Robert was my pal. My work was covered in a day or two.

I was still wholly invested in new clubs and nightspots. I was to be seen in one every night I was not working, dancing all the time. I was not big on the spirits; I liked whiskey, but not vodka or gin. Then there was a Portuguese sparkling wine called Mateus Rosé, like Prosecco. Everyone drank sparkling pink wine, and they drank gallons of it. I danced it out every night and I became very well known for my dancing. So much so that, every time a new club opened, I got free membership because basically, I was the entertainment. I had no problem getting up and dancing alone. Just wind me up and set me off. If I heard music, I had to dance. It was like being in red shoes. I would dance so much that I would take a change of clothes. I would be so soaked in sweat that I would change half way through the night. Not a single piece of video of this exists. It is a bit saddening as I was just mad, Mad.

I had some wonderful dance partners. One such was Benito Carruthers, a big American snaky kind of guy. He was an actor who would later play in *The Dirty Dozen*. He was a fabulous dancer. We would get on the dance floor and we would clear it. I loved him, he was wonderful. He had been married to but separated from Leila Goldoni, a friend of mine, an actress, also fabulous.

It was the 1960s, and everyone was 'doing' everyone else. It was the era of sexual liberation and I was sexually free. The animals were let out. It was just wonderful, there was such a freedom. It was a whole lot of fun, and I felt completely free to do what I bloody well pleased. There was a lot of sex going on at that time.

By this time, I was friends with Michael Caine whose girlfriend was Edina Ronay, and Michael's best friend, Terence Stamp. We would all hang out together and we would go to a party. Just before we entered a party, I remember Terence saying, 'Let's give it a moody' whereby we would present as all moody and pouty. It was a bunch of us having a lot of fun in little gatherings and pockets of people. I would sometimes disappear for a weekend with another group of artists where we would get together to spend the days smoking and dancing like idiots. And it was not necessarily sexual. We took flights to Paris for the weekend to find and take whatever drugs were in fashion. It was madness and I was loving every minute of it. Whatever you wanted to do, you would just do it.

## 1963 – 1964

I didn't have to audition for the part in *From Russia with Love*. Terence Young had earlier said to me that he had an idea. When the James Bond film was being prepped, Terence came up and said, 'You are going to be my gypsy girl.' This was around the end of May, or maybe early June. I was supposed to be going to film in Turkey so I went to Pinewood Studios to sort out all the passport requirements. But then, Turkey was cancelled for me and the whole gypsy camp scene would be filmed on the Pinewood Studios back lot. I think it had something to do with Pedro Armendáriz, the gentleman who was playing Ali Kerim Bey, being very ill with cancer. So, the producers decided not to take us to Turkey.

My scene in *From Russia with Love* was the fight in the gypsy camp between me and another female gypsy and the later shoot out. I was to play Zora, and Aliza Gur was to play Vida. In the story, we were both in love with the same man, the gypsy chief's son. To prepare for this scene, we rehearsed the whole fight in Pinewood Studios. It was three solid weeks of rehearsing to properly learn to fight. Terence wanted to have the fight fully choreographed as he wanted to use handheld cameras, and to come in close on us. We had to be able to repeat all of the individual moves from any point in the fight. A stuntman taught us. I am not sure it was the film's stunt arranger, Bob Simmons. He might have set it up and passed the responsibility off to one of his team. We spent the three weeks, Monday to Friday, in a rehearsal room fighting and learning to fall on mats. It was during the rehearsals that I met Sean Connery and did all the publicity photos with him and the gun. I liked Sean. It was interesting again to see immediately that Sean and I would have a good relationship. There was mischief in his eyes. You could see it right away. Some of the publicity was released while we were rehearsing; the press was full of, Bond Girls Fight, and, Battling Beswick.

We finished the rehearsals and then visited the set. It was huge. It was a whole gypsy encampment where they filmed a belly dancer, some entertainment and Bond continuing the mission with Kerim Bey. And then the encampment is attacked. The filming went really well. It was cold, it didn't rain, it was in June, and it was filmed in the early am, not late pm. The filming took a week or 10 days for the whole scene, including our lovelorn girls' fight.

Information around the internet has me as having been Miss Jamaica. As I mentioned earlier, I have never won that crown. However, Aliza Gur had been Miss Israel. Neat and petite, we got on as workers but we were never sisters. Having met the other Bond girls at events and parties, we are all each other's sisters. Something didn't allow us to be good friends, but we were good at what we did and were committed to doing a good job.

*From Russia with Love* was my first major film, if not a major film role. So, it was unfortunate that in the opening titles as created by Maurice Binder, my name was spelt as Martin Beswick. No 'e'. My name is correctly spelt in the closing titles but not where it would have been of more importance. I realised this only when I saw the film. I don't think I bothered to ask them to change it and anyway, how could they have? I never went to the premiere, which meant my involvement with the film all took place during the rehearsals and the filming of our scene.

Sean and I got on very well during filming and he suggested my voice was perhaps too Jamaican and he recommended me to his voice coach called Cecily Berry who, he felt, would really make a difference to my voice. I went to see her and we worked a lot; not just on my accent but also my voice. She was a fantastic coach. She made my voice come forth. I worked with her for several classes over the course of a month or so, sometimes with a couple of other people. And to be sure, my voice certainly became a whole different thing. I had never worked on my voice before, and then I think with tutelage it got deeper and bigger. It made me aware to not to speak from throat, but from the diaphragm. And it became The Way. I saw Sean again with Terence for a dinner or party and thanked him again for the recommendation.

I never met Robert Shaw. I loved his scene with Sean Connery on the train because it went on for so long and with limited dialogue; both playing cat and mouse, back and forth. One of my favourite scenes in a Bond film.

As well as paying for the voice coach, I moved from Connaught Square and rented a flat in Seymour Street near Marble Arch; a large two-bed flat in a very lovely apartment building. I have no idea what I had been paid for *From Russia with Love*, and in fact I cannot remember what I had been paid for any of the films. Bizarrely, I do remember what I had been paid for the secretarial work.

Many years later in May 2012, Stephanie Wenborn from Eon Productions invited me to the Cannes Film Festival to introduce a screening of *From Russia with Love*. It was part of the 50th anniversary of the James Bond films. I was so surprised, and utterly thrilled to be invited to such an event. I had never been on the red carpet. I was paired with Bérénice Marlohe, who had played Séverine in the soon to be released *Skyfall*. She was so beautiful and charming; she held my hand as we walked over the rain-soaked carpets and stone pathways. The world's media were everywhere taking photographs. Bérénice and I had cocktails, after which I introduced the screening of *From Russia with Love*.

The Bond sisterhood was still very present even though our respective Bond films were so far apart. I was amazed I was doing this as my part in the film was not exactly the main character. But the thing is, a Bond girl is a Bond girl. It was a lovely two days. There were fans at the airport waiting upon my arrival, and it was the same when I was about to leave.

The whole Bond fascination never ever ceases to amaze, thrill and surprise me. I am so glad I have my Bond sisters to play with.

## ■ MUSIC / FASHION / LONDON

I was enjoying London to the fullest extent. But it was not hard to enjoy the city. This was the era of the Beatles, the Rolling Stones, Motown, Stevie Wonder; the music was so rich and so wonderful. London really was the centre of the world at that point. London was portrayed on the cover of Time Magazine; Swinging London, it really was. Each of the music groups and names became massive stars. It was an incredibly exciting time for music, and I loved my music from the days when Mummy played everything from Frank Sinatra, to Perry Como, to classical, to Blue Danube. When mum played the Blue Danube, I put on my ballet toe shoes and tutu, and insisted on performing for her and her tea guests, and to get rid of me because I just couldn't stop, she paid me two and six pence.

I saw lots of concerts. I used to love Traditional Jazz. It was growing in the 1960s. There was an enormous amount of different music, it was insane. My money went on buying records. There was a place in Marble Arch, a record store. I went on Saturdays and got to know the guy who owned it so well that he knew what I liked. He would find odd stuff. I would ask him what he had found. I bought it, took it home, popped it on the gramophone, wore my headphones, and I would go mad and dance. If I was depressed, I would indulge in the music. Music was important to me. Another great place to buy music was in Harrods on the top floor. It was a record store, fashion store, and café called Way In. All the Young Things gathered up there to hear some new music, where you could listen to the records in booths before you bought them. We would listen, have a meal, drink some coffee. It was truly an exciting time for discovering all types of music.

## ■ TIME OF LOVELY YOUNG THINGS ON THE BRINK

At the same time, there was an enormous sense of freedom which we felt completely entitled to. It kind of led to not just freedom of thinking and fashion but also to bed hopping. We were all randy little animals just leaping about. There was something about that that we didn't really think too much about, or too deeply. The rules of the game were, you had fun, and if it ended, you would get a bit sad because you wouldn't play any more with that person, but then you'd move on. There was at this time never A One. You just moved on from one person to another and continued the fun. As an example, Albert Finney was a very desired playmate, very much desired by all. He was at the top of the Desired List. He was one of the people who had just come into their own. Finney had just done Tom Jones, and he was fun. We met each other in a club called the Crazy Elephant and we had a delicious affair that lasted for about three months. We were very badly behaved. We were in a restaurant where we decided to recreate a scene from *Tom Jones* between Finney and Joyce Redman. It was a scene where the two of them were eating at a table opposite each other, but it was like they were having sex. The food, the kissing, the noises. Everyone started looking, and then laughing, and then applauding. All very good fun. And when it ended, it was what it was. He had affairs with two or three of my best friends. Theirs were longer. And this was just what happened, the rules of the game, everyone was leaping on everyone else. Sometimes, but rarely, they would even move in with each other.

However, I did meet someone, again in the Crazy Elephant. He was gorgeous, a dancer, he looked like Marlon Brando, and he knew it too. He pursued me, his name was Michael Wade. Against all the odds of the era, we became boyfriend and girlfriend; a regular thing that lasted for about a year. He had a business partner whereby together they bought properties to either resell or make housing developments. By the time we met, they were trying to get hold of Albion in Jamaica. The coincidence! By this time, my grandfather did not own it any more. Michael and his partner were due to go there to buy it and to make it into something. I'm not sure what. In the end they didn't buy it and instead went off to San Francisco towards the end of 1964 to look into a particular property.

I had some gift for extra sensory perception and by this point, it was really high. I would have dreams that were predictive, astral travelling, genuinely wild times in terms of my spirituality. Michael was in San Francisco and I dreamed that he was in a discotheque that had purple onions for tables and chairs. I assumed it was called the Purple Onion. In my dream he was dancing with this girl who looked a little bit like me, I tried to go up to him and tap him on his shoulder. 'What are you doing?' I asked in my dream but he didn't or couldn't react. And I couldn't do any more than what I was asking of him. I called him the next day and spoke to him. I asked him if he was in a club called the Purple Onion. 'Yes,' he said, 'How did you know?' I told him he had been dancing with this girl and asked him what he thought he was doing. Well, this really freaked him out. It turned out that he had struck up a relationship with this girl and she had followed him back to the UK. He no longer spoke with me. And later, he married her. Many many years later, I met him again and they were no longer together. He said, 'You ruined my life. Why? Because I thought of you as a witch.' Perhaps this was because of the astral travel and all that I had related to him about that. I admit it was all a bit weird; I did not know what to do with all this. I also liked his sister, a beautiful intellectual. And I knew and I was accepted by his family. I can't say I was truly in love with him and I think this was why I bounced back from this relationship quite quickly. I knew there was a lot of fun still to be had. Yes, I was angry by his behaviour, but I made it all go away. I knew my ESP was rampant at this time; I kind of trusted that side of me to help me get through it. The ESP and the dreams and astral travel went on for years. It was a strange time. Sometimes I would be picking up so much that I had to leave whatever environment I was in as it was too painful. I had a great friend who knew about this stuff. I went to him and asked, 'Can you help me?' 'You must not be frightened of this as it will make it more difficult,' he said. 'Relax into it and it will be fine.' And I did. Unfortunately, I have not experienced this lately. This is a shame it might have helped me win the lottery, which I live in hope for to this day.

## AMERICAN FILM BUSINESS IN LONDON

The Americans were central to the film business in England. They were all here in London; the Producers, the Directors, and I met some of them. One became my dear friend, Michael Mindlin, a film publicist. He introduced me to all sorts of people, one of whom was Elizabeth Taylor who was quite gorgeous and lovely. This was a whole other tribe that I was entering into. The American film people were so numerous that they had set up a baseball game in Hyde Park for every Sunday. It became quite famous; it was also a really fun social time for everyone. You had to be in with the In Crowd to be there, and I was. It was an afternoon thing as clearly, no one gets up early on Sunday mornings. They would have the game and then follow it up with eats and drinks. I was introduced to a producer called Martin Ransohoff. He had a bit of a bad reputation but I liked him. He was producing a film in Paris called *The Sandpiper* with Elizabeth Taylor and Richard Burton. Also filming in Paris at the same time was *What's New Pussy Cat* with Peter O'Toole and Ursula Andress. Pete and Richard were great drinking pals and I found myself hanging out with these people. The two films came together and they undertook a huge PR campaign in the Hôtel George V in Paris. Everyone was there; the magazines, the newspapers, the press and I found myself to be a part of that group. It finished, we walked out, everyone had been drinking through the day and Peter, in one of his mad moments said, 'Give me your shoe.' He took my velvet slipper, poured the champagne into it, and drank out of it. We ended up going to a club, utterly drunk. I was sitting on the stairs with them, talking together asking of myself and them, how did I get into these things? Insane.

The producers had brought me in to be an extra on *The Sandpiper*. This had been because I knew both Michael Mindlin and Kaffe Fassett, the son of the founders of a very famous restaurant in Big Sur, California called the Nepenthe. The director was Liza Minnelli's father, Vincente Minnelli. Kaffe Fassett was in Paris as a consultant to advise on the verisimilitude of a set that had been constructed to look like the Nepenthe. It is for the Taylor and Burton scene. There are Greek dancers, and it is my big moment to dance with other luminaries behind the table holding Burton and Taylor. Filming in Paris is superb, as you only started filming at around 12pm, maybe to finish around 8pm. What this meant was that there was so much more time for drinking.

And all this happened because the Americans ran the film business from London. To be sure, the UK at that time offered tax breaks to bring American dollars and filming to the UK, and yes, they loved to use our technicians. And notably when they left in the early 70s, it was bad; there was no work whatsoever.

## ◼ 1965 – 1967: THUNDERBALL

In 1965 Terence Young was once again my champion when he insisted that I was the right actress for the role of Paula Caplan, Bond's liaison in the Bahamas for the next James Bond film, *Thunderball*. Harry Saltzman was very opposed to the idea, as he did not want any Bond Girl to appear twice. He was quite rude about it; so rude in fact that the words are positively unrepeatable. I almost had to laugh he was so rude; a man I considered to be a coarse and rough diamond. I only heard about all the exchanges after the decisions had been made. Terence had made the argument that the character was an Island Girl and I was exactly that. He won! Why look for somebody else when you have the perfect island girl. For some reason he felt I was right for it. Of course, the part could have been played be somebody or anybody else. All this happened before we left for The Bahamas, in April 1965.

The Bond films had been growing globally and *Thunderball* truly was the zenith. Every top magazine converged on the island and the publicity shot the franchise to a greater world-wide status. Claudine Auger, Molly Peters, Luciana Paluzzi and I all became great friends. I was not working every day in The Bahamas. As both my co-stars, Claudine Auger and Luciana Paluzzi were working every day, I was assigned to doing an enormous amount of publicity on behalf of the film. That was my job, virtually every day. What this meant was that, even though I was not working and acting, I was the one that got all the publicity; I was even on the cover of Look, purely due to the others' unavailability. Playboy was also on the island. They had previously chased me for other work unrelated to James Bond. I had said No. The film's on-set publicist set up this engagement. There gathered this fairly well-known Italian Playboy photographer, me, and couple of others. We got on a boat and went off to shoot some photographs on a sand bar or a small island. A minute patch of sand, there was nobody on it. When we arrived, the boat and the other people took off and left us there. Just me and the photographer. He said, 'Take your top off.' 'No.' We fought and argued for a bit. I was angry; the bastards had left me on this island with a man who was imploring me to take my clothes off. 'Fuck you,' I thought. I ripped off my top and said, 'Ok, go.' I was pissed off; they had trapped me. I was moody for the photographer but what else was I going to do. For many years later, Playboy kept coming back to me offering ever increasing amounts of money. I said no, I was not doing it. I was still that angry with them. And anyway, there was absolutely no way I was going to take the bottoms off. All this contrasted with some minor publicity I did before any of us went to The Bahamas. I went to Pinewood Studios and, as by then I had not laid on a beach for two weeks and suntanned, they had to slap the make up on me to make it look like I had a tan. And the results were not good.

I enjoyed the filming. I was still very early in my career and quite green. I think what Terence saw in me was my Jamaican spirit; I wasn't going to put up with any shit. The scene in the film where Sean and I are in the boat after he has just introduced himself to Claudine Auger's character, Domino, Paula's character is clearly not impressed with Bond's method or success of introduction and without the respect so deserved of James Bond, I say, 'Well I don't call that contact.'

It was good to see Sean again; both his wife and his son came out to The Bahamas to be with him. I adored Diane Cilento; she was bawdy, a really great spirit. She would tell these wild stories over dinner. I was a bit of a fan; she was gorgeous and fun. And so too was Jason a delight. During the filming, we all lived in a group of houses that were all together. Sean, Diane and Jason were in one house. Rik Van Nutter and his wife Anita Ekberg lived in another house nearby, she was pretty amazing too; a big spirit, one not to cross. The film company had hired a guy who gave the best massages. He had been an FBI agent and he had the biggest hands I had ever seen. He used to massage Sean at their house. And after he was finished

with Sean, I would then get a massage. I would arrive at Sean's house, open the door to be let in and upon seeing me, Jason would take all his clothes off and run around. It was hysterical, it happened every time I arrived. Evidently there was something about me that inspired him to be naked in my company. He was an adorable little blond kid.

I was working a few days on, and a few days off. There was an occasional night shoot. My schedule was completely random, unlike that of Sean's or Claudine's where they were working all the time.

Much of my time off set was spent hanging out with Terence, Sean, Diane and the producer, Kevin McClory and his wife, 'Bobo'; Frederica Ann Sigrist, who was the daughter of Sir Frederick Sigrist, the aviation pioneer. I loved Kevin, he was properly Irish and very much was a part of the mischief set. They all had these specific looks on their faces when they were beginning to get up to no good. I was in with the right crowd. I am not sure the producers and Kevin were the best buddies. I didn't understand all that, the dynamic and how they had introduced themselves to each other but I was having fun. The dinners at the weekends were huge. Kevin was part of the wider experience for extravagant dining. So much so that after we had finished and went back to London, Kevin invited us all to a christening in Ireland. He flew the whole group to Ireland where we proceeded to spend the most drunken weekend any of us had known.

*Thunderball* was my biggest film thus far and I was having fun. I even had a boyfriend. Barclay 'Buzzy' Warburton owned a beautiful sail boat called the Black Pearl that featured briefly in our film. Buzzy became my lover. I realised *Thunderball* was a huge film, but I can't say I was really fazed by its enormity. This really was just another chapter of fun. I once gave an interview which then became titled, 'It's all about the fun'. And for me it really was. If I am not having fun, I am not doing it. I loved being with everyone, I had great friends, and the friendships are a key ingredient in my life; deep long friendships. When I meet someone and I like someone, I say, 'Too bad, you're hooked now.' I love my people; I couldn't possibly see how I could live without these people in my life.

Filming in The Bahamas wrapped and we returned to Pinewood Studios. I had to do a couple of interior scenes including that of my character's death and I think that might have taken roughly a week.

After filming on *Thunderball* had wrapped, along with Honor Blackman, Pussy

Galore in the previous Bond film *Goldfinger*, Molly Peters and I were flown to Rio de Janeiro to represent Bond at the city's first Film Festival which was to be attended by many international Stars, Directors and Producers. I have no idea how it happened for us to be sent there, I just found myself there. It was all to generate more publicity for the world of James Bond. *Thunderball* was the turning point where Bond was up and away, and there was no turning back. Even though Rio had never held a film festival before, it nonetheless attracted the likes of Warren Beatty. He was really naughty, but also, he was hilarious. He had a reputation, and it was something that he had to keep going to perpetuate the myth. This guy had an amazing memory; he would remember where we met, when we met, your name and he was truly well known for that. I liked him and he was fun to play with. Unfortunately, I did not get to 'go there' because in times past I had said No.

The Festival was fun. We were interviewed, we attended film premieres but there were a couple of particularly mind-blowing events. Molly and I were all staying in the same hotel, but in separate rooms. We decided we would like to lie on a beach for a bit, so we collected our towels, went down to the beach and no sooner had we lain down than we were surrounded by young men shouting 'Bond Girl, Bond Girl.' It was an unsettling situation and it reminded me of a scene in a film with Elizabeth Taylor, Katherine Hepburn, and Montgomery Clift, called *Suddenly, Last Summer*. Clift plays a character who finds himself on the beach with a bunch of young boys. They attack him and eat him. And this encounter immediately felt just like that was just about to happen to us. Oh My God, we were in trouble. Luckily, the security team saw us leave the hotel and rescued us again, but it was really scary.

We met Antônio Carlos Jobim. He had written the Brazilian bossa nova and jazz song, *Girl From Ipanema*. He was really cute and he decided he liked us. He invited us to his hilltop villa in Rio which was lovely. It was just Molly and I. We all giggled a lot. It was wonderful, we were flirting and he was singing to us. Then we had to go back to the hotel. Along with another friend of his, he drove us back and escorted us to our rooms where they then tried to force themselves upon us. We could not believe this was happening. We both turned into fishwives, Molly and I, and we went into a complete madness. They both ran off. It had been a wonderful evening, and then this happened.

We had another very scary incident. We arrived at a film screening at the Film Festival in a limousine with Adolfo Celi, Molly and me, and we found ourselves being rocked in the limo by fans who were screaming, Bond Bond. Again, it was really scary. A Security team had to step in to disperse the fans and to get us into the cinema. It was the only time I had ever experienced that level of fandom and made me really feel for the super stars like the Beatles, who regularly had to flee from that kind of madness!

The Premiere to *Thunderball* was held on 29th December in London's Piccadilly Circus at both the Rialto Theatre and the Pavilion Theatre. I attended with John Richardson who was wearing the beard for the film, *One Million Years BC*.

My sister was still working as a private nurse. But as a side line she had started to design clothes. I had backed her and set her up in the second room of my Seymour Street flat. For the Premiere, she designed a beautiful white gown for me.

## ONE MILLION YEARS BC

I had been hired to play Nupondi in *One Million Years BC*. Because of *Thunderball*, I didn't have to audition for the part. I didn't speak to anyone at Hammer Film Productions; I was contacted by my agent of the time at William Morris, a man by the name of David Booth. They organised the whole contract, and I don't remember meeting anyone from the Hammer gang until I stepped off the plane in Lanzarote.

However, I was by now having second thoughts about doing *One Million Years BC*. It was a time in my life that my Extra Sensory Perception was very strong and my dreams were at times very predictive. I had been seeing photos and newspaper articles of John Richardson and my reaction on viewing him was very strange; the experience would leave me shaking and physically disturbed. I somehow knew that if I ever met him, my life would change in a way that I was not ready for. I was having far too much fun. John was to be the star of this film.

Pictures of John were everywhere. Just prior to *One Million Years BC*, John was filming *She* with Ursula Andress and the publicity was rampant. I later saw him in a restaurant in London that everyone was going to and I nearly fainted. 'Oh my God he is so beautiful. But I can't ever meet him.' I knew that my life would irrevocably change and I was just not ready for it.

I tried to break the contract when I was in Rio at the Film Festival. I had met the Italian film producer, Dino de Laurentiis, at the Festival and he was in the process of setting up a new film. Maybe I could get a part in that so I could not do *Million*.

I spoke to my agent to see if I could be released from *Million*. I did not mention why or that it had anything to do with John. I realise this all sounds ridiculous, but I felt so strongly about it.

David approached Hammer with the request, but they came down heavy on me and threatened to sue me! So, I flew out to Tenerife to join the cast and crew. John and Raquel Welch had been filming for a week in Tenerife and were about to transfer to Lanzarote where we would be working for the next six weeks. I landed at a small airport and was greeted by Michael Carreras, the son to the Hammer founder, James Carreras. He was at the foot of the steps of the plane.

"So, you decided to make it" said Michael with a winning smirk
"Well, I am here" I replied, returning his smirk.

I was carrying two small cases, my record player and my LPs which he graciously took from me. We entered a very basic airport building and at the other end of the building was John Richardson. Our eyes met and there was an instant electric connection. I can almost feel it now, just talking about it. Everything just stopped and we stared at each other. Neither of us were remotely 'cool'. When we got nearer to each other, the feeling was almost like, 'Don't touch me.' Michael was witness to all this and he later said he had never seen anything like it before.

We all flew on to Lanzarote, we arrived at the hotel and got our rooms.

The first night, dinner was with Michael, his wife Jo, Don Chaffey the director, John and I. The connection between John and I was palpable. There were some more friendly snipes from Michael about my having tried to remove myself from the contract, but we got to banter, which quickly continued to us becoming really great friends. He was also witnessing the literally electric sparks between John and I.

It was impossible. The next night we gave in and were in bed together. It was pointless to try to resist it. I had a boyfriend in London, but honestly, had I been married I would have been in exactly the same trouble. I had by then already decided that marriage and children were never to be in my life, but perhaps living with someone could work. My life as I knew it took a whole different course. We fell madly in love. It seemed he was to be my destiny. He was renting a flat from Lady Elizabeth Clyde, with whom he had had an earlier affair and with whom he was still good friends. I would stay with him at his place. I got to know Elizabeth

61

Clyde and her sons, Jonathan and Jeremy (the latter about which, more later…). I was now no longer bed hopping or dancing every night, as from this point on, we both went from film to film. My life had changed on every level. John had become central to my life. My earlier fear had been that my life would change, but once it had changed, and I accepted that, I succumbed to the inevitable and was madly in love and absolutely obsessed. John had had several affairs with older women. I was his first younger one and that literally floored him. Of the two of us, he was the bigger star. He was eight years older than me, and contracted to Rank Films. So even though I had been aware of him and knew exactly what my reaction to meeting him would be, he had been not aware of me and had therefore no prior reaction to any images of me. Until we met.

Lanzarote was fabulous. It was so wild; no wonder they were filming there. There were no high-rise buildings as is now the case. The locations were fantastic; one location of which was a pea-green lake right on the coast surrounded by the volcanic black sand and the Atlantic Ocean. There was an incredible rock formation surrounding the lake. El Golfo is an emerald green lake on a black sanded beach that was the consequence of a volcanic eruption. The colour of the lake is caused by a semi-precious stone called Olivina that can be found amongst the grains of the sand.

When we had to stand in the water for some scenes, we noticed that water at the top was cold, while the sand that we were standing on was hot. We filmed a huge scene there. Ray Harryhausen was the special effects wizard who created all of the stop animation dinosaurs. I absolutely adored Ray. I only met him the evening after That Dinner. As his work to make the monsters would occur after we had filmed the live action scenes, he would direct us exactly how and where we had to fight monsters. He would stand on the back of a flatbed truck and, with his special stick that he would use as a baton, direct us. It was a very funny scene as we were all holding spears and stabbing at thin air. There were times when it became so hilarious, we would all break down in laughter. We also shot the scene where Raquel's character is taken by a Pterodactyl; a scene that gave me a perverse thrill as, in the film, John was my man and Raquel had spirited him away from me! I was so happy that she had gone, even if she was to be later rescued.

Filming *Million* was amazing. In the film, John and I were part of the Rock tribe. We were dirty and grubby cave people. Raquel Welch's character belonged to the Shell people; they were pretty, wore make up and knew how to use utensils. One scene had the Cave people going hunting where they caught and brought back a

pig for later cooking and eating. For the filming and because we had to be seen diving in to the pig and grabs pieces off it, they actually roasted a pig on the set. First the men, then the women, and lastly the children got to eat. We sat there like little animals attacking the food. It was really hot, but delicious. We made for very authentic cave people.

The film called for a fight between the characters played by Raquel and me. It had not been rehearsed so the production brought in two stunt people who would perform the fight. Raquel and I were sitting in our chairs watching the two stunt performers. Raquel and I weren't best friends as such, but we worked well together, and we respected each other. We looked at the two people, turned to each other and said, 'No Way. We are going to do this. You can't film these two people as they look nothing like us.' We were both dancers, so the stunt coordinator was called in to choreograph the fight. Another outing for Battling Beswick.

There was one scene in *Million* that was cut out of the American print. It was a sexy dance with me dressed in my bits of leather. I had taken something to drink, the drums were beating, and I went into this mad sexy cave woman dance. I don't know why it was cut; I was fully clothed, or at least covered.

We filmed in Lanzarote for six weeks and then returned to the UK to film a bit more in the ABBC film studios. I enjoyed working on this film and I liked the finished product. And John and I were very much besotted with each other; I had accepted my fate.

A few days after our first dinner in Lanzarote, Michael said, 'I want you to be my Queen in my next film, *Prehistoric Women*. We will shoot it right after *Million*.'

'Tell me more,' knowing full well that I was definitely going to say Yes. 'I need a new wardrobe of leather and I want to wear make-up like Raquel is wearing.' Michael was totally dead pan, utterly brilliant. He said, 'Carl Toms will take care of your costumes.' Well, there was no argument there, as Carl had designed Raquel's fur bikini for *Million* and went on to win awards for set and costume design in other film productions. All the sets from *Million* were kept and redressed for *Prehistoric Women*.

Within weeks of finishing *Million*, we went into filming *Prehistoric* in the same studios. Michael Latimer was a lovely guy, but I wasn't sure if he was right for the role or the film, but we really worked well together. However, my dear friend,

Edina Ronay, was my co-star; she played the goody blonde, me the baddie brunette.

I knew exactly what I was going into with this film, and I fully subscribed to it. Michael and I would start, 'I think what we need to do…' and no matter what we did, it would contain liberal levels of sexual innuendo. 'Do we really need to do this?' And we would start laughing. Michael gave me some great lines. I ate them up and threw them out. It was my film and I was here to have fun. It was all filmed in the studio with stock footage to suggest we had visited and filmed in Africa. I had Steven Berkoff imprisoned. I murdered Carol White. I took it all seriously. I loved working on this film. I fought and danced through my film. The whole cast went for it and it was completed in six weeks; a long shoot for a low budget film, especially as all the sets had already been made. I also brought my sister in as an extra. It was all a wonderful experience. However, the film was what it was and the reviews were not positive even if one of them said of me, 'She makes a good bitch kitty actress.'

Later in California, I was on a low budget film called *Cyclone* along with several other well-known actors, including Martin Landau, before he had received his Oscar. Between set-ups, we competed with each other for our respective worst film. *Prehistoric Women* was mine, except that now, it has attained cult status.

John and I were very much in love. As he wasn't working at the time and he was friends with Michael, John did the on-set photography. He was a lovely photographer and very good with women.

## ■ JOHN AND I SIGNED FOR WESTERNS

John and I were both coincidentally signed for spaghetti westerns that would both film in Spain and at the same time. John was to star in *The Tough One* which would film in Madrid, and I was to star in *A Bullet for the General* which would film in Almeria. Mine was a big film in very much the same vein as the Clint Eastwood spaghetti western films. We were both asked if we could ride horses; we both lied. We realised we needed to do something about this, as we would be looking forward to months on a horse. There was no, 'Maybe we don't need to do this.' We decided to go to Hyde Park to take lessons. We had never been on a horse, much less ridden. It was not long before the English saddles had our butts bleeding from all the jigging. I came up with an idea; I bought some sanitary towels. Both of us were wearing them in our knickers. They saved us, we continued to learn. Luckily when we got to our respective filming locations, we found the Western saddles were divine; they were like sofas. The productions had also supplied trainers to get us in shape. Probably they were supplied secure in the knowledge that a majority of the actors would have lied about their abilities to ride. Anyway, within a week, my handsome horse, Tarzan, fell in love to the point of him getting a hard on or rather, a long on for me. The crew found this hilarious. Poor Tarzan was very embarrassed.

*A Bullet for the General* had a good cast. It had a German actor, Klaus Kinski who was amazing, and a fantastic rider. It also had an Italian actor, Gian Maria Volonté who, again, could also ride, and a Swedish actor, Lou Castel. I was the only woman. Damiano Damiani was the fantastic director, and I think he made a pretty good film. It also became a favourite for my fans.

There was a lovely man known as The Baron who rented apartments to the stars. I have no idea as to his nationality or even his real name. He was not Spanish, but perhaps Eastern European. Next door to me in the same apartment complex was Clint Eastwood, who was finishing the filming of *The Good, The Bad and The Ugly*. I had visited him on his set. The Baron was a kind and gracious character who really looked after his tenants. John was working in Madrid and we missed each other terribly. We were desperate to be together. Baron organised a taxi to drive me to Madrid after I had finished shooting on the Friday. The journey took eight hours over night. I would get to Madrid on the Saturday morning and we would spend the Saturday and Sunday together. And then on the Sunday evening, the driver took me back to Almeria. I did this journey many times over most weekends. I was supplied with a blanket, a pillow and food. Baron had vetted the taxi driver to guarantee he would take proper care of me. I was filming for three months, and I did this nearly every weekend. John couldn't do the journey, as by now he had incurred a bad back.

There were times we had to film scenes with extras, gypsy extras. We all had to get on a train to move to another location. I loved these little interludes as, during the journeys, the gypsies taught me how to sing, and how to do the flamenco clap. Before the filming had commenced, Damiano, the director, had shown me around Madrid. He took me to a bull fight which I initially found to be awful and which later I found it to be amazing. Then he took me to a flamenco dance. It was a wonderful venue, a cave. The dancer was a beautiful young man, and he performed this incredible dance. He was so fabulous; I couldn't believe just how exciting it was. He turned around, he whipped off his hat. It was a woman. I was in love.

## ■ THE PENTHOUSE

Peter Collinson was a director who had done a lot of TV. John's old school mate was John Naylor, who was married to a very lovely Indian lady, Ina. Whenever we were invited to their house, Ina always cooked us the most wonderful Indian dinners and foods. Any time dinner was offered, we could hardly wait. They were always elegant and delicious, and their guests were always great people. Peter was one of them and it was at one of these dinners that I met him. With buck teeth, we immediately bantered; he had a wonderful sense of humour. We met up a few times and right out of the blue, he said, 'You know, when I do my first film, you will have to be in it.' 'When,' he asserts, 'When I do it.' Although Peter later went on to direct *The Italian Job*, his first feature turned out to be *The Penthouse*. On the one hand I was relaxed about going into this as I already knew one of the principal actors, Suzy Kendal. On the other hand, this film was a five hander, meaning the screen responsibility was divided equally, five ways. This completely freaked me out. It would place far too much focus on me within the duration of the film. 'I know you can do it,' he said, 'Have a read.'

I thought, I can't do this; this is serious work. It was an odd film, full of odd characters. 'Peter, I really can't do it.' 'Pull yourself together,' he finalised. It was a claustrophobic set made to be an apartment. The entire film was made in this one set. I played an insane degenerate under the cover of a probation officer. My character is called Harry, and I am in charge of two other degenerates called Tom and Dick. Tom, Dick and Harry, that was sort of the madness of it all.

Five actors in all, the two other characters were a young woman who was having an affair with a married man. The married man is the manager of a building of apartments; all of which are unoccupied and to which he had easy access. It is in one of these unoccupied apartments that he is conducting this affair. In my role as a probation officer looking after the two ex-cons, we find out about the affair and, under the guise of gas meter inspectors, we decide to terrorise them. We were horrible. In fact, the film was to have originally been called *The Gas Men*. We give the woman drugs, the guys rape her, and I take it upon myself to slap the adulterer about. The whole thing was quite horrid; the subject made me very uncomfortable. Pretending to be a probation officer who is fucking crazy, I had to find a way to play this role while not giving anything away too early as to my craziness.

If this was not bad enough, my very first scene to be filmed was a five-minute take; a monologue. I was shaking in my boots. But I got through it somehow and

I did a good job. And that was at the beginning of the film. In retrospect this film was the best thing that could have happened to me, as an actress. Peter came from live TV, so he was used to focussing on a character and filming close ups. But to me, this was very new. As it happened, each of the five actors had their five-minute scenes. But, mine was filmed on my first day without resorting to any adlibbing. I was lucky to be blessed with a photographic mind where I would see the words on the printed page, and they were immediately in my head.

Filming took only four weeks. Although the three protagonists could be seen as the affair couple's conscience, everyone was fucked. The message being, if you do wrong, you're going to be punished. But we all were awful characters, and everyone was unpleasant. Perhaps unsurprisingly, the reviews summarised as, 'An unpleasant little film.'

John was in Europe at the time seeing people to progress his photography. There was no way we could not be together if we were in the same city. We finally got a flat together even though there were discussions about us going to LA. We chose a place in Thurloe Place, near Harrods. John was also very close to his family. He was an only child whose family lived in Sussex; we would often pop down to see them at the weekends. I loved them, especially his dad, a gardener and a very proud man.

John and Dini Leyton were old friends of John Richardson and so we all became a tribe where we were to later share many adventures together.

## ■ LEARN TO DRIVE / VISA / GREEN CARD

John had a house in California and we both had money. We thought, 'Let's take a look at the house, maybe sell it, and buy something together in England.'

At this point, I did not drive. Not being sure how long this process would take, it became obvious that I could not rely on us having only one car and me on John to drive me around. This was California, the distances are huge, and I would have to drive my own car. While in London, I did not take public transport, I just took a lot of taxis and so I never had to drive. In LA, I would be even less likely to take public transport. I started my driving lessons. I took to it like a duck to water and passed my test first time.

We had been working nonstop while in London. There seemed to be no reason to think this would stop even in LA. If I could work. For this I needed a green card. Even though John had dual citizenship, we weren't married and so I needed to acquire the documentation to work. It took a whole year to sort out. We started the process in January and received it all just before we left. John also had to write a letter guaranteeing that if anything went wrong, he would be financially responsible for my welfare. I am aware it is now much tougher to acquire a Green Card. I am very glad I did though because subsequent to that, I became an American.

## ■ SISTER

I said earlier that I had worn a dress designed by my sister, Laurellie, to the premiere of *Thunderball*. Still working as a night nurse, she had decided to start designing and making clothes. Her idea was for creating really comfortable jersey dresses and pant suits whereby you could fold up a whole wardrobe in a suitcase. I thought it was all fabulous; I was impressed and so I backed her and set her up in my flat in Seymour Street. I gave her my second room and a sewing machine, and she worked hard. The problem became that she was now working very hard on two distinct areas of industry. I started to see what it was doing to her; she had begun to shake. She was working all night, she wasn't sleeping and while she was not a drinker, she was taking uppers. I saw the signs; I had been there.

My sister had been seeing an older American writer who was a bit psychotic. The problem was that when my sister fell in love, she would listen to everything they said and it was the same with all the people she fell in love with. She would listen to only that person's words and opinions irrespective of the benefits derived from other's opinions and for a more balanced view.

Before it really began to hit her, she had an incredible fashion show in Dolly's Club, a big club in Jermyn Street. I knew the owners. Marilyn, Alex, and Esther all modelled the clothes and it was pretty fantastic. My sister sold clothes to Fenwick's on Bond Street and she also gained her first big client in Jackie Collins, sister to Joan. Laurellie and I started going to parties; we were called in magazines, 'the sisters from Jamaica'. After that, she went downhill. I was getting ready to leave for California and still she didn't want to hear anything from me. This American man was her Svengali.

Suddenly she began to get really shaky. 'It's nothing, Nothing,' she would say. 'Let's just see a doctor,' I said. I took her to a private doctor on Harley Street whereby he suggested a sleep cure similar to what I had been assigned while in Jamaica. She was on the very edge, her nerves were shot, and it had been four or

# THOSE SISTERS FROM JAMAICA

Martine Beswick, who made a big impression in Thunderball, has since made Slave Girls and The Penthouse. While Martine's movie career is swinging, her sister Lorelei is branching out into a different field. Fashion design. She started off by designing some fantastic outfits for Martine, and from there everything snowballed. Friends who saw Martine's skin-tight cat suits wanted to know where they came from.

LORELEI BESWICK (above)

more months without regular sleep or food.

However, her 'handsome and brilliant genius' told her, 'You don't want to do that; the effects will limit your creativity.' I was so angry and upset. My sister said that he was right and she would do as he suggested. I tried to argue with her, but there was no way. He 'knew' what was right, and he had my sister's ear. I left for California having not been able to achieve anything for Laurellie.

After a few months while I was in California, I received a report from a friend. My sister had been admitted to hospital and diagnosed as a schizophrenic. I was not able to visit her, as now, I am the evil one. She does not want to see me. I keep getting reports from friends in London to suggest she has had electric shock therapy and that she has been released from hospital under supervision. Finally, I had to go see her. I caught a flight to London but upon seeing her, it was awkward. My beautiful sister was now on really heavy drugs and she had put on weight. Prior to all this, Laurellie had been really funny, truly hilarious, but now she had become almost sombre; squashed because of the drugs. In one respect the American was right in that the drugs would adversely affect her creativity. These people hate being on the drugs, because their creativity is lost, and so they come off the drugs and the problems recommence.

I went back to Los Angeles, and the reports kept coming through to say that she was in hospital and then out, in and then out. She started writing terrible letters to me; I was sad and angry. If she had had had the sleep cure, I believe that she would not have been pushed towards what became her high levels of bipolar and schizophrenia. In times of comparative peace, she once said to me, 'I would not wish this illness on my worst enemy; you have no idea how horrible it is.' I saw her again later, when she was having one of her episodes. She felt that 'they' were coming to get her, she was looking through the window, she was waiting for 'them' to come. It was a mania that made her fearful of what was going to happen to her, and who was around her who might harm her. It was just awful, heart breaking to watch. I felt really helpless.

By now the American had left her and she was now in an intellectual love with her doctor. She was always drawn to people with brilliant minds and her doctor was a lovely man; he was fantastic and had a great sense of humour. They had a lovely relationship. It was not a sexual kind; she was just in awe of the great mind. It was always all about the mind, nothing sexual. That was mainly her thing. For example, I didn't have a big enough brain for her. She fell in love with brains; it was not just about being in love with the person. And her doctor, he knew how to take care of that side of her, which made her admire him even more.

It was in this way that she went on for the rest of her life. In and out of hospital; in and out.

## 8

## 1967–1972

# CALIFORNIA, LEARNING MY CRAFT / LIFE AND LOVE

John and I left London for California. We arrived in Los Angeles to John's house, a lovely little three-bed house with a garden and a fountain. I found it all really exciting. It was a new place with new people and maybe new horizons even though the idea was to stay for an unknown quantity of time to ensure the selling of his house. California was huge, very different and really cool. My mindset was that we would be returning to the UK but three months had passed and nothing had happened. Suddenly, it seemed easier to maybe just stay here. I was not terribly happy about not going back to London but then Eliza Clyde moved to LA and lived just up the road from us on Beverley Glen. Then John Leyton and his wife Dini arrived. This was a big deal. John Leyton was an actor and singer and between them, Eliza, and John and I, we ended up in going from house to house to socialise. It was hilarious; we had a lot of laughs.

I began working. I became the little woman; I became a great cook, a gardener, a decorator. My days included putting together dinner parties. John introduced me to his first family, Thomas and Simone Hormel and their tribe. I was welcomed with open arms.

Happy days with John Richardson and I

75

## ■ ACTING CLASSES

I started acting classes.

I went to Stella Adler, another coach who founded the Stella Adler Academy of Acting & Theatre in Hollywood. She was tough, really tough. She had a class of about 30 people. We were again asked to choose and prepare something to be later acted out in class, and I chose something really stupid. It was a scene from the 1960 English kitchen sink drama, *Saturday Night Sunday Morning*. The scene had me in a slip, ironing as a wifey. To this day I do not know why I chose it; it was certainly not me. It was a bad choice, and on top of that I acted it badly. At end of my performance, Stella looked at me, she picked at my clothing and said, 'What is this, this piece of cacca!' She completely ripped into me. I was almost brought to tears. I thought, I am not going to cry in front of her. But I was thoroughly embarrassed; I had been demoted right in front of the rest of the class. But you know what, she was absolutely right. I had not hit the mark and I had let myself down. I breathed heavily. She said, 'Give me something else.' I went away and came back with a monologue from the 1959 film, *Suddenly Last Summer*; this same film of which I had been reminded by my episode on a beach in Rio. The scene enacted the moment when a friend had been eaten on the beach by a group of marauders. I gave it everything I had. Stella sat there watching me with tears in her eyes. 'That's what I want to see; that is Exactly what I want to see.'

That was unbelievable. It had been something to hook into that I could portray, and to do so in such a way that people could see what I had to offer. And I knew all this as I had been performing the scene. So, I never did that again. Other things certainly hurt me in my life, but Stella killed me. It was the start of something though, something that had been hammered in me.

I saw in a newspaper that the New York based Lee Strasberg Acting Institute was opening a school in LA. Purporting the Acting Method, I joined, and it was the best thing I ever did. I did some serious learning. My tutor was the fantastic actor, Peggy Feury. New Jersey born, she was an actor of Broadway, film and television who herself had studied with Lee Strasberg at the New York based Actors Studio. Lee had suggested that Peggy and her husband, Bill Traylor, move to LA to create the LA branch of the Strasberg school. Lee himself would come in to the LA school for three months of year.

The first day I joined, I was sat in the studio, I was really excited and this guy walked in. Our eyes met. His name was Michael Taylor and he turned out to be my first ever soul mate. We became instant friends to the point when, after class, we would have lunch together three or four times a week. John Richardson was my destiny; Michael was my soulmate. Michael was gay, and he introduced me to his boyfriend, Neil Dillard. We all became life-long friends. He was generous and caring; he became many things to me. We communicated in ways where we didn't even really have to talk. I might mention a word as if to begin a conversation, and he would just nod and say, I know.

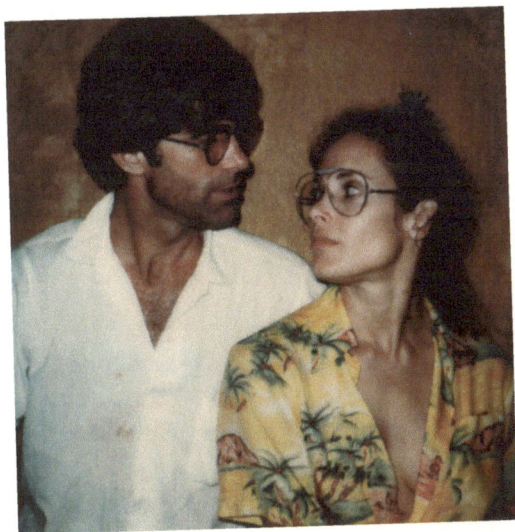

Soulmate - Michael Taylor

A number of other actors and actresses attended the school to expand their work and their skills. After class, four of us would go to what quickly became our favourite place, a restaurant called Musso & Franks Grill. Created in 1919, I still love going there whenever I am in LA. A great place with red leather booths and that which was host to all the film industry. Film stars included Greta Garbo, Gary Cooper, Humphrey Bogart and Lauren Bacall. In the 1950s, one would see Marilyn Monroe, Joe DiMaggio, Elizabeth Taylor, Steve McQueen, Jimmy Stewart and Rita Hayworth. It was the same in the 1960s. We would have a Welsh rarebit and get completely drunk. We'd sit there all afternoon discussing the classes, acting, and films. We would end up blottoed, go to someone's house to sing and dance, and then do it all again the next day. Those were very different times where we drove drunk. As soon as we got behind the wheel of the car, we sobered up for however long it took to get home. And then carry on. Musso's holds many good memories.

The classes were fantastic. They were challenging. We would be told to choose a scene, we would rehearse it, come back to the class and perform it. And then Peggy would pick it to pieces. We would be told where we were not getting the right flavour, and whatever was not working. It was brutal and full on. And if it was not right you would have to take the criticism. Some people would break down over the critiquing if you were rotten, or even if you were good. It was also terribly exciting when you magically hit that moment; you would just sense it and think, Ahhh brilliant. They are the moments that keep you going. If you don't get those moments, you may as well bury yourself. The training worked in two ways; it made you a better actor but it also toughened you up quite considerably.

She was the first coach that I worked with. I later worked with Lee for a month which was equally really intense. He still ran the studio in New York where everyone who was anyone went through to perfect their craft. I kept oiling the machine. When you weren't working on films, you kept going to Lee or Peggy. They were two of the three fantastic coaches that you went to. They pushed you into areas of thinking that you might not ever consider if left to your own devices. They pushed you out of your comfort zone. By way of example, into small theatres, and I am not a theatre girl, I am a film baby. You really had to work hard. It was really exciting. You would discover things about yourself that you did not know. One of the coaches said, 'You are going to do *Macbeth*.' And I did!

I did a solid year of acting classes at the Lee Strasberg Acting Institute. I did not work for films or television during this training. I had so much money from my work in the UK and both John and I wanted to avoid some of the inherent taxing. We got an accountant and formed these companies to get around the taxes.

My company was called Best. John's was called Fair. We were still just a bunch of kids having a good time. I bought myself a Mini Cooper S. It was the last one to be brought into California; they had been considered to be just too small for the American roads. It was speedy. John had previously bought a Ferrari from Rome and had it shipped to California. The bloody car did not like traffic. As soon as we hit any, it bloody stopped. In the end we sold it and bought a VW Camper Van for his photography equipment.

We were enjoying life in California. Our friend, John Leyton, had just done a TV series. He and his wife Dini rented a house on the beach. Whenever he needed to come into town for an audition, they would stay with us. And then we would all go to their house for the weekend. I was still playing the little woman at home.

78

I was interior decorating, I was gardening. I grew Gardenia shrubs and marijuana bushes; the flowers hid the bushes. We called our house the 842 Club simply because it was the address of the house. 842 Beverly Glen. All of us were into a bit of gambling. One particular Christmas we went to Las Vegas in John Leyton's yellow Rolls Royce. We practised some gambling before we went. I did not like blackjack, however I loved roulette. John played Craps, John and Dini played elsewhere and I sat at the roulette wheel. Separately doing our own things, we all won! The casino staff brought us drinks constantly until 3am. As we were gambling, our rooms were free and we won thousands. I won $2k, my John won $4k and John and Dini won $2k or $3k. It was also our last night in Las Vegas. We got in the car to head back to LA. We were 50 miles out of Vegas. We were very quiet because of the rapture over our winnings, and then we saw a merest sprinkling of snow in the distance. Well, since we of course couldn't possibly get through those climatic issues, we turned back to Las Vegas, and played more. And lost everything. We laughed at ourselves for a long time. It was hilarious. I guess we were doing this because we thought we were invincible. We were obviously not millionaires, but we felt like it, and behaved like it.

I was still with the William Morris agency but they did not really represent in LA and LA did not know who I was. I had to resign from William Morris in 1968 and find LA representation. Again, through John Richardson, I met Robert Walker. He became another champion in my life, a darling friend and a hilarious man. He had been involved in structuring John's contract when he was with Seven Arts Productions and was loaned to Hammer Film Productions for *One Million Years BC*. Robert opened his own agency, Century Artists, and I was his first client. I had taken a further step back from London. Robert was lovely. At the beginning of his agency, he would actually take me to auditions. Something that was unheard of.

This was at the time when Sharon Tate was murdered. John knew Sharon very well. We had been to the same house where she was murdered just the month before. When it happened, the whole of LA was experiencing random murders, not just Sharon, and it created a lot of very scared people. LA was in shock and we did not know if any of the, let's say, 'rich and famous' were on The List. After that, everyone flushed their drugs down the toilets in case of police visits and searches. It was incredibly sad and awful. Sharon was gorgeous and sweet. That was not a good time; it put a black cloud over the city.

## ■ WORK

My first forays into working in LA were in television and all through Robert Walker. In 1969, I did one of the first episodes of Universal's, *It Takes a Thief*, with Robert Wagner and Liliane Montevecchi, a brilliant classical modern dancer and was a star of her own show in Las Vegas. She was also a dear friend of John's and so she became mine too. She had also swum the English Channel. It was a lovely first experience. Everybody welcomed me, and treated me well. I never felt like I was undermined or put out, and Robert Wagner was terrific, really divine.

I then did in the same year an episode of *The Name of the Game*. This was a TV series that had three rotating stars who featured in different episodes, all held together by a common theme. They were one and half hour episodes as opposed to the standard hour-long format. This was special. The episodes were a little meatier. Directed by Sutton Roley who was to later become another one of my champions, my episode starred Gene Barry as an FBI agent, and the story was based around the Cuban Missile crisis. My character was involved with people surrounding Fidel Castro. The story had Gene's character and mine fall in love. Gene had earlier said that, 'the episode could not have Martine as she was too young.' But Sutton supported me; he said I had a Cuban look and that I was right for it. It was a really good and terrific piece; it turned out to be a truly meaty role that took about 10 days to film.

In 1970 I did another TV episode, this time for *Mannix*, a long running Paramount television series that had Joe Mannix, a private detective, use brute force to solve crimes. The lead character was played by Mike Connors who I had briefly met in Rio and with whom I had had a little flirt. The crew was lovely on the whole; I had terrific experiences even if I was new in town. First of all, it took a while to get going, thank God I was learning and now working. I was getting to know the craft and the acting studio kept me going, even with not getting all the parts. I was so absolutely obsessed with being an actress and if I was not working and I happened to pass a studio, I automatically thought, 'Oh my God, why am I not in there?' I loved all the studios; I did a lot at Universal, 20th Century Fox and Paramount.

In 1971 I did the pilot to what became a one-season TV series called *Longstreet*. The premise to the series was of an insurance investigator, Mike Longstreet, played by James Francsiscus, who was recovering from an explosion that had killed his wife and had taken his eyesight. Deciding to remain an investigator to solve crimes, he also wanted to find who was responsible.

This was for me, a big one. The opportunity came about due to a meeting rather than audition. I didn't receive the script until the last minute when, by then, we were on location in New Orleans. I was loosely primed, and I was aware it was a pilot. Written by Stirling Silliphant, he was better known for and had won an Oscar for his screenplay in 1967 for *In the Heat of the Night*, and which starred Rod Steiger and Sidney Poitier. *Longstreet* was his first TV series. The director, Joseph Sargent, was also well-known for having directed the film, *The Taking of Pelham One Two Three*. The cast was fantastic; it was a first-class project.

We had all flown to New Orleans, the filming location. My character was Nikki Bell, his assistant who taught him braille and became his eyes during his investigations. When we arrived, we went straight into rehearsals before shooting. It was the first day and I was a bit stunned by the seriousness of the piece. I knew that I had had no time for preparation, but because everyone else had by then received the script, they had all had the time to digest it. I felt really small. They had all been cast before me, and I had been a last-minute casting. Sterling was very much for me being in the role, a level of support that might not necessarily have been mirrored by the studio. I think that is possibly why I was cast last minute. In the world of television, to be cast you have to jump the hurdles of both the Studio and the Network.

We were still in the rehearsal room, and I was feeling shitty. 'Ok,' I think, 'that's it. I've got to get this together.' Everyone went to dinner, and I stayed up all night and I did my homework. The next day, in the rehearsals, everyone's eyebrows went up. Maybe they had been thinking, was she going to be the right person? But after that day, people came around. James had been stand-offish. We had to get this together, we had some intimate conversations and suddenly we were shooting. It had started to work, we were talking to each other, and discussing how we were going to make this work. The relationship had started to form; it was really great. And the relationships between everyone else now also began to form and consolidate.

New Orleans has a real feel. There is so much history there, the slavery, the Mississippi River, the music. You just could not help feeling the history; it grabbed you. Every bar had wonderful jazz and blues music playing. We all felt it. We filmed the first scene in a cemetery, there was a lot of spirituality, the voodoo, the mix of all the people; it all leant a true feeling to the scene. I loved it.

We also shot in an amazing plantation house that had these incredible and gnarly trees with the draping Spanish Moss so evocative of New Orleans. It had an incredible energy.

And so, the filming went really well. Everyone was very happy with it, and James Francsiscus and I were in great shape. We returned to LA and awaited the approval from the Network for the series to go ahead. From LA, I went to London for a few days.

We returned to LA to the news that the series had been green lit but that I had been thrown out of the series. Why? Stirling was apoplectic. Why? Because, they said, 'She's too sophisticated for American audiences.' Maybe. Being of Jamaican and British heritage or descent, I was known as an exotic. But I think there was another consideration. It was evident that James and I started to have a very solid on-screen relationship. It was real, and I think that was just not what they wanted. For the first episode of what became the only season, they cast Marlyn Mason who was a really good actress but did not exemplify the relationship that I had had with Longstreet. In the film, I was more of a colleague where my involvement was more intense. Perhaps that way was too sophisticated, but either way, I felt shit. Stirling went in again and fought for me but he couldn't win. The Powers, the Studio and the Network all have to have their say, and the Network is the worst of all the barriers to get through. Perhaps they wanted just one star in the show, and not two stars. Maybe. Or, they just did not want an assistant having a meaningful relationship with the lead. But to my thinking, I was the key to the eyes. I never saw the show. For our pilot, the writing was good, the directing was good, the actors were good; it was a class project, until it wasn't.

This one hurt a lot. That was going to be my 'In' to a meaningful career in acting. The series lasted one season, but it would have been a huge feather in my cap and a good money earner.

*Night Gallery* was a short-lived American TV series not dissimilar to *The Twilight Zone*, both series of which were written by screenwriter and producer Rod Serling. But whereas *The Twilight Zone* series focused on science fiction, *Night Gallery* aimed for the horror and macabre. I cannot remember whether I auditioned for this role or not, but that I can remember anything at all is in itself a miracle. We shot the entire episode in one continual 24-hour working day. My episode was called *The Last Laurel* and starred Jack Cassidy. The premise of the episode had Jack's character as a crippled athlete who uses mind over matter to commit murder. Taking place at night, all the actors were dressed in pyjamas. To this day I have no idea why we had to film everything in 24 hours but all of us were falling asleep on our feet; literally falling asleep. I was good at sleeping on set when not required but this experience saw me falling asleep when required. It really got me. The episode was a three hander which also starred Martin E. Brooks and was directed by Daryl Duke. Filmed at Universal Studios, it was all a blur, a nightmare; something that had never happened to me before or since. The most bizarre experience of my life; I had never heard of anyone else having to go through that. Your sleep pattern goes nuts. I had done night shoots before; my first night shoot was for *From Russia with Love*. But then, I was younger, and I was used to staying up all night. But as I got a bit older, and as by then I was in a relationship that precluded all night dancing, it got a bit more difficult.

It was still 1971, I had just finished *Longstreet* and I popped over to London for a short holiday and to see some friends. It seemed a nice way to celebrate what at the time I had been sure would have been a greenlit and long-term TV show. Stirling Silliphant, the show's writer and my champion, was also in London. We had dinner, we chatted, we were figuring all would be great, we were waiting for the positive responses and we were excited. Even though I had left the William Morris agency due to being in LA, I had maintained a friendship and I went in just to say Hello.

I was immediately greeted by the words, 'They are looking for you, for the film *Dr. Jekyll and Sister Hyde*.' I started laughing, 'You mean Dr Jekyll is going to turn into a woman?' I liked the idea. I went to see Michael Carreras of Hammer Film Productions and Brian Clemens who wrote the script and concluded that this could be interesting. I was always of the opinion that we all have some male and some female in us. In the film's case, those elements were written to be out of balance. I always thought the male within me disproportionally rose up every now and again. I think I realised at some point that not only had I some male in me, but that I was an alpha male too. And I think too, had I had a penis, I would have put it around just as much as all the guys; I know that. So, using that information in my head, this film I thought could be interesting, and the character interesting to play.

There was no audition; as I was in town, I just went to meet the director, Roy Ward Baker. Because I had been working, and I had done the acting classes, I was ripe for another meaty part; I was ready. I had a lot more tools in my toolbox for my craft. I started thinking, I started to sizzle and cook. The role required nudity when Dr Jekyll morphed into Sister Hyde. They specifically wanted to show Sister

Hyde looking in the mirror at her newly formed breasts. And then, when she is disturbed by the upstairs neighbour who walks through her door, realises the power of her breasts over the stunned man.

I understood the importance and agreed to it. I had been in London mainly for a little vacation of a few weeks. I returned to LA to the crushing blow of the *Longstreet* decisions and I came back to London for six weeks filming of *Dr. Jekyll and Sister Hyde*.

We started shooting and was surprised by the sudden demand of full-frontal nudity. My back went up. Roy Ward Baker was a lovely man who I believe was being pushed by Hammer Film Productions to make the demand. Hammer were going through a period of nudity in their films which for me was the beginning of their demise. They took the nudity too far. There had always been a suggestion or a hint of nudity, but now it was all full frontal. Anyway, there was a big hoo ha; they saying they needed it, me saying no because it wasn't in the script and hadn't been agreed to. Now I am furious and so I start playing up. 'If we are really going to do this, then I need a merkin!' Essentially, a pubic wig. The point was, I did not have a lot of hair down there and I did not want to be completely exposed. The film's hairdresser was involved. As she measured me, she became completely embarrassed. And this carried on for a while. 'They are just not going to get it,' I told myself. The process was a big 'fuck you' to Roy, or at least the Hammer people who had been forcing Roy into this position. But it got to the point where I then said, 'Ok, this is not going any further, we are not gonna to do it like this. No more merkin; we will figure this out another way.'

The scene required me to be wearing a dressing gown and walking in a room towards a curtain. I had then to remove the dressing gown, arrive at the curtain, pull it down and wrap it around me as if it were a dress. Obviously, this was not going to be a problem; I was envisaging doing it in one take. I arrived on set to find that they had positioned the fucking camera on the floor and pointing it right Up me. I was again furious. Off we go again. I shout, 'You Cannot film me from down there.' While the rest of everything said does not need to be recorded here, finally they moved the camera to a more accommodating position. I had attended toga parties for years and was fully experienced in the art of wrapping sheets around me. It took one take and actually, the scene as filmed and edited was a triumph.

I never had an issue with nudity on film. Contrary to how this may appear when thinking about the event in The Bahamas when I had been spirited away to an island for some PR photography, the problem with that was not because I had an issue with doing it, but how they had engineered me into that position. I hadn't wanted to do the nudity in The Bahamas because I was angry by the way they had left the photographer and me alone on an island. That was a shitty move to leave me on the Cay without even a publicist to accompany me. The nudity in 'Hyde' was essential to demonstrating the bodily changes, so I was fine with revealing and showing my top half. It turned out to be an interesting scene in the sense that my character was shown to being reborn. I looked at myself in the mirror, I looked at my breasts, a guy from an upstairs apartment opened the door to my apartment, I turned around, I didn't really know I was a woman, he was shocked, I discovered my Power over the man. It was a key moment for Sister Hyde whereby I see that I have these breasts and they are my power.

After that, I think I had earned a reputation for being difficult. But I think, fuck you all. Don't fuck with the Beswick. Many years later, we were watching the film with Brian Clemens and Roy Ward Baker for a commentary track for the film's DVD release. Roy said that in retrospect we could and should have really explored the sex changing more deeply; which was exactly what I had wanted at the time of filming. Certainly, we had managed to show a little bit of the depth to the psychology of it all, the confusion as Dr Jekyll touched his face during the physical change, but it could have been much more.

It had been a six week shoot all at the studio. There was no location shooting. All the exteriors were shot in the studio; the entire thing filmed in a stage. Aside from the nudity issue, the set had a really good atmosphere. Brian Clemens poured everything into it. There were lots of people and characters from unrelated books and films; he threw them in the film too. Naturally, me turning into a murderess is right up my alley; I have to kill in order that I continue to be. It was an interesting character and I think one of my best performances. I was shortly after in the south of France at the Cannes Festival with an old friend. We were having a drink and he said, 'You are in Variety, you've won the Festival Prize for best actress for this film.' He later delivered it to me in Rome.

I didn't really do very much publicity for 'Hyde'. There were nice reviews. I think it was key for the producers that on some level, Ralph and I looked alike. We didn't really but it was like when one owns a dog, and after a period of time you start to look alike. We thought that that was what happened. We had the same outfits;

we had the hair the same way and no one had thought of taking a photo of us wearing the same things. 'Hey, hello, shall we take a damn photo like this, both of us in the same clothes.' The photo was taken and is now very famous.

Many years later I met Brian Clemens at a show or a convention. We started flirting, it was again just as hilarious and as mischievous. Brian's wife was divine too. When Brian died, Caroline Munro and I attended his funeral. If these things can be described as such, it was the best ever funeral. It was held at his church in the country. Everyone had turned up including his wife, Janet, and his two fantastic sons. They had asked several of us to say something and before we got up, the priest started talking about him. Within minutes, he too had us laughing at everything Brian would have said.

It was our turn. Caroline and I always played off each other and we told our personal and loving stories of Brian. The whole church was laughing again, because everyone had also experienced Brian's innate humour. It turned out to be a true celebration of this man. Sure, there were tears later in the pub, and then there was laughter again. He was adored. He was a joy; the funniest man in the business. I realised I had gathered these people around me all of whom exhibited the same kind of mischievous look; Terence Young, Kevin McClory, Sean Connery, Michael Carreras.

## ■ BEGINNING OF GAY TRIBE

I had met Michael Taylor at the Lee Strasberg Institute and had become instant friends; we were very much attached to each other. Upon meeting him, I hadn't realised he was gay, and even if I had it would not have made any difference. All was fine. Michael had a lover, Neil, and the three of us became great friends, becoming in the process completely attached to each other. We couldn't do anything without each other.

Michael was 6 feet 3 inches and gorgeous, a real power house. It didn't occur to me that he and his friend were lovers and that they adored each other. They were guy guys. Michael was very male. Indeed manly. So too was Neil. Michael was an actor and model. He also wrote a book called *Male Model*. Neil was a singer. I was with John Richardson so I just got to know Michael and Neil. These were the first couple of gay guys with whom I became such good friends. It was not until later that we began to play. And to play in ways that as our group widened and as my friends were the most important part of my life, would lead to heartbreak.

## ■ JONATHAN DEMME

Another person who needs to be introduced now for later embellishment is Jonathan Demme, the director who later became well-known for *Silence of the Lambs*. Evelyn Purcell was an Australian friend of mine. We hadn't seen each other for a couple of years until I bumped into her in 1965. She was the assistant publicist on *Thunderball*. We became best friends and through her in London, I met the other Australian girls. She went to New York with Eon Productions to promote Thunderball and it is in New York that she met Demme. They had a relationship, they moved back to London, I had moved to LA and, while I was away, they got married. I caught up with Evelyn and Demme when I popped in to London for '*Hyde*', and so we hung out together. It became a different gang. I was still with John Richardson who was still in California. I was still in touch with Evelyn who by now was bizarrely being called Maud. Apparently, she called everyone else in the world, Maud, and so, by way of payback from her friends, She became Maud. Leaving 'Maud' in London, Demme came to LA for a film and so I suggested he stay with us. He came to produce a film called *Angel Warriors*. Originally called *Angels Hard as They Come*, it was to be directed by Joe Viola.

At my invitation, Jonathan came to stay with me at the 842 Club as he had no money and I had a free room. At that point I met his team, his director, and 16-year-old Gary Goetzman, child actor and music contributor. They completed the film and just as quickly left to set up other films with producer partner, Roger Corman. They had started their own company and started many actors in their low budget films. I was still in LA, but I came back to London and we became friends again.

## ■ JOHN RICHARDSON

He was in London with me when I was shooting '*Hyde*'. Again, he took on-set photos of the production. It was around now that he had started to stray. I already knew what the problem with John would be. He was a very beautiful man and to women he was like a magnet. We would go to parties together and he would say, Don't Leave Me. He would have to handle this himself as I was never going to be in his company for 100% of the time. But the women would talk to him briefly and then literally drag him into a bush. And I would know it had happened, every time. I would wait, and finally he would confess deeply to me. It was all very weird because I knew he really loved me, knew what he was like, and the women.

Maybe it had started before we came back from London, every now and again but after we returned to LA, it became more frequent. When John and I, and John and Dini were together, we were inseparable. There had been no messing about. John had gone to Spain to film *A Candidate for a Killing* with Anita Ekberg. It was not long before I started hearing stories of the two of them having an affair, even though her husband, Rik Van Nutter, was with the two of them. This was a final straw of sorts. How did that test my resolve to be faithful? There was a certain moment. I was best friends with Jonathan Clyde and his mother. I met Jonathan's brother, singer Jeremy Clyde at an amazing studio owned by Thomas Hormel of Hormel Meats. The family, his wife Simone and four children, became my family. Thomas' studio was equipped with incredible sound reproduction equipment. There were huge mirrors on one wall and, hanging from the ceiling hung four sets of headphones. Being able to then play the music as loud as we wanted, we would then all dance in front of the mirrors. Jeremy and I flirted madly and we became bad babies. As in, we had an affair for a couple of weeks.

We had arranged I would visit John in Spain, and I was riddled with guilt on plane. I met John and of course I knew exactly what had been going on. Rik had been watching it all, and now too so was I. But Anita Ekberg, she was a force to be reckoned with. Now am pissed off. I could have had more fun with Jeremy.

Our relationship was now not in great shape by the time we get back to LA; something had come in and destroyed us and our relationship. And very rapidly, it all went further downhill from there. He went off to Rome to find his spiritual self. My friend Jeremy fell in love with someone of whom none of us approved, even though she was really quite lovely looking.

John's experiences in Rome had made him decide to sell up in LA and go to India to meet Mother Theresa and photograph her for a special presentation in the Sunday Times Supplement. He told me about his amazing acid trip and I told him that I had also had an incredible acid trip with Michael, and we had sex. He was furious with me. Really? He was permitted, but not me? For some ridiculous reason, I agreed that we would both leave LA and return to London after which he would go to India for his photo assignment. You can imagine, I was not pleased.

I was not at all sure about going back to London as I was now becoming a hot commodity in LA. However, very quickly, we sold everything including the house, which he sold to Barbara Parkins, a well-known actress and an ex-girlfriend of his. I had put a lot of my own money into this house and if I was to set up in London, I would need that money back. I was promised £10,000 once we got to London and the money had come through from the sale. He took the VW camper; we got on a boat to London whereupon he told me to wait for him. He kept all the money and disappeared to India which was an insufferably selfish move.

Barbara Parkins had a flat in London. She needed someone to look after her cat, Pushkin. As I had nowhere else to live and no immediate other choice in London, I took her up on it. I had not been to London for years; I had to reconnect, I needed to see my friends in London. I found Esther first.

I had been working as a model which took me to Amsterdam and Germany, and luckily, I was making decent money. He asked me if I could pay to fix his camera. I was hurt and angry at his request, but for some idiotic reason, I agree to pay for the camera repair. Shortly after that, he announced that he was going to Rome for work. I was livid. 'You do that,' I retorted. That was the fucking end; he had been so selfish. Even his father had told me, 'Don't you wait for that selfish bastard.'

It was a bad and sad time actually. It had been an incredible love that we had had, but it had been so completely destroyed by his selfishness and disrespect; it was really terrible. Many years later, he came to see me. 'You were pretty awful you know, you left me with no money,' I said. It hadn't even occurred to him. In retrospect, we left LA together as I hadn't really felt we were finished, but it was a stupid move on my part. In relationships, there is always a period when you Should have left, and yet we still hang in there. Maybe it could be better, or, maybe we were not finished. This was one of those moments.

This was the same moment when the American Film Producers had all left the UK due to a new tax regime which no longer favoured the American or British film industry. There was no work. I thought about going into theatre. I tried but all the names that were usually doing films, were now doing theatre. So, for me, getting in was an impossibility, hence why I went back to modelling.

And then I received a call.

It was John Richardson. 'You have to come to Rome, there's loads of work here.'

# 9

## 1972–1974

# ROME, WORK / LOVE

---

### ■ JOHN RICHARDSON SPLIT

I arrived in Rome and my agent created a publicity opportunity to promote both me and my presence in Rome. A statement to say, 'I am now based in Rome and I am ready to work.' We went to a restaurant in Fregene which was a beach resort nearest to Rome. As it was out of season the restaurant was completely empty. I was sitting with photographer and the publicist awaiting the completion of whatever else had to be set up. I was happy just to take in the surroundings; it seemed the restaurant was not completely empty. At the other end of the restaurant, there was another group who looked to be doing something similar to us. As part of that group, there was a well-known PR photographer, and a guy. Our eyes connected and simultaneously, it appeared we were both absolutely freaking out with attraction for each other. Who is that? He and his assistant came over to my table and immediately, he and I were in absolute madness; we were shaking. I was still smoking at that point and I tried to light a cigarette. My hands shook. The man was an actor and he was called Maurizio Bonuglia. My publicist was well-known and well-connected. He had access to a house on the beach that he offered to us for our photography. Maurizio came with us to the house. It was impossible to keep our hands off each other. He kissed me while I was trying to get the photos done. It was mad, it was passionate, it was fiery and delicious. We had such an indescribable connection to each other that we initially could not define. After several weeks, we both volunteered that we had known each other in another life, and that it was in that other life that we hadn't worked out as our love had been forbidden. Life after death is just something I believe in and so too did he.

John Richardson heard of this and was furious. 'How could you do this to me?' 'We are not together,' I replied. 'Now go away.' He was incensed that I would have found a new lover, even though by now he had had affairs and we had long since separated. To this point, I had been living in a pensione. There seemed to be work in Rome and I had a lover. I decided to move from England. Maurizio found for me an apartment near Piazza Navona. It had a fireplace and it was just divine. I returned to London to collect some things and to finance myself. By this point, I did not have much money, but I had a lovely bank manager, Mr Deeley. He became my dearest friend and he was also very good at 'finding' money for me. I went to see him to enquire about a loan. A lovely man, he seemed to have none of the checks and balances required for the making of a loan; he gave me some money and he hoped that I would repay it. I bought things for Rome; cushions, sheets, odd things. I packed it all into crates and got on the train back to Rome. What was I thinking? I arrived at the train station in Rome but I had no idea how to get to my new flat, as Maurizio was not in town. Providence supplied a truck driver in the vicinity of the station. I could understand a bit of Italian. He saw me surrounded by my crates. 'Do you need some help? I can take you to wherever you need to go.' He lifted all the crates on to the truck and he seemed to understand where it was that I was trying to find. He seemed quite nice, friendly, unassuming, and he had not propositioned me. We found the flat, unloaded the crates, and took them up the stairs and into the flat.

'Now, what about a little something?' Evidently, I was still very much in Italy after all. 'Oh! I trusted you, how could you?' I was very put out. I played it up and made a major performance out of it. It got to him; he became very contrite and backed away. I paid him and off he went. At least he hadn't jumped on me.

I was now based in Rome and with a new lover. We had fiery fights about anything and everything. It was all part of our relationship. He had a wonderful flat and we ended up in spending a lot of time at his place. He would pick me up for mad loving sessions; wild, animalistic, it had to continue, we had to hurry up, we had a desperation for each other and for it to happen. If I had been thinking that I wanted to see him, he would just arrive, such was our connection.

## ■ SEIZURE

I was still in Rome and my agent, Robert Walker, called me to tell me he had a script written by Oliver Stone originally to be called, *Queen of Evil*, and that he wanted me to be the Queen. I was interested, but then the weirdest thing happened. I had been staying at a friend's house near the beach. One night I had a terrible nightmare which featured a giant and a dwarf standing next to me. The giant was threatening me, and the dwarf was standing to my side. The following day I received the script and, in the story, there is a giant and dwarf! My heart started beating and I thought that this isn't good; this can't be right.

I had another nightmare with the giant and the dwarf. No, no. Robert called me to say that Oliver really wanted me. There wasn't a lot of money attached to the project; in fact, it was scale, minimum wage. I reread the script and I did find it interesting. I could make the role mine; it would be my film. So, even though I was still a little scared, I said yes.

The film was being shot in the US so I flew to LA. Before we moved to the shooting location I stayed with Robert in his house. I had told Robert my weird dreams and the weirdness was to continue. We were both reading script over dinner and Robert was thinking about who could we cast in it? We were laughing, it was all good fun when suddenly, there was a huge crash on the street below us. Robert's Beverley Hills drive was steep. We exited his house to investigate. Across the bottom of his driveway, a car had crashed into a tree. We walked to the car and sitting inside was a dwarf.

Robert and I looked at each other. What on earth was going on? It was not a small car but it had been made to fit the driver. Robert invited him into his house to rest up and await the authorities. He was an actor, and there and then, Robert decided that he would be cast in the film. I cannot believe what had just happened, and what Robert had just done. I took it in my stride. We called someone to move the car. In the end, it did not work out for our crash victim as, when Robert finally spoke to Oliver, it turned out that he had signed Hervé Villechaize, an actor who found later fame in *Fantasy Island* and *The Man with the Golden Gun*.

Everyone boarded a flight to the Laurentian Mountains in Québec, Canada, just north of Québec City. Oliver Stone had organised as the main location a huge ranch house which sat adjacent to a big lake. We were picked up and taken into the country where we met everyone. The ranch house served not only as the filming location, but as the production's living accommodation. It would be a short commute, but it also meant that we would never be able to escape each other.

Jonathan Frid had the lead role as a horror novelist who is subjected to recurring nightmares about three characters from one of his books who terrorise both him and his family. The dream then becomes a reality. Frid had the main and master bedroom, and I was next door to him. The rest of the cast and crew were spread out throughout the rest of the ranch. Everyone would wake up, make their own breakfast and clean up after themselves. Together with this, all the film equipment was stored in everyone's bedrooms. Jonathan was quite grumpy about having to sleep amidst so much film equipment, but we did have a laugh about it. A normal film shooting experience, this was not.

The premise for my role was to take vengeance on a variety of people; I was people's murderous consciences. Troy Donohue was my first victim; I seduced him and then murdered him.

Behind the scenes, the dramas were developing. The make-up and Special effects man was an alcoholic. Called Tom Brumberger, he would drink himself into a stupor and not make the call times. I took it upon myself to get him up in morning for work. In the end, I brought him into my bed to keep an eye on him. He was cute but nothing could ever have happened as he was always drunk. He was a mad person.

Hervé and Oliver formed a relationship which went beyond the film, and later we would meet up together in LA and they would turn up for dinner, both dressed in velvet suits and smoking cigars. Quite a sight. Hervé was lovely and one of the stars of the film, Mary Waranov, and I were his favourite laps to climb on to, and he had our permission. He was a very bright and interesting man.

Then we started to the think that the house was haunted. We were shooting in the attic and I was trying to find and kill a child. It was a dramatic take. We were on the roof and from nowhere, hail stones as big as golf balls started crashing on to the roof. We had to stop filming. Also, no one could use a sink, shower or toilet while filming as the house's crazy plumbing noises would otherwise ruin all the takes. Then, whenever there were filming requirements for any night time exterior scenes, suddenly, the cameras would just freeze.

The crew's drinking became a little excessive. There were gallons of wine available. Then Hervé heard his wife had had an affair in Paris. He went mad. He took to carrying a knife around with him and in violent fits of rage he stabbed the table tops.

Oliver's wife was lovely. At some point in the shoot, she returned to New York.

Oliver and I were getting close. I saw him as a genius. Nothing happened between us but, for the last scene, I was preparing in his room. In a fit of unwarranted jealousy, my drunken make-up and effects friend, Tom Brumberger, picked up an axe and tried to chop the door down. We heard him coming and we pushed a huge chest of drawers against the door until someone heard the raucousness and held him off.

We filmed for four weeks. We all returned to Montréal and said goodbye to everyone. Oliver stayed in Montréal to cut the film and I stayed with him and we had a short but intense affair. It had been brewing while we were filming. I did think Oliver was on the brink of big things. A couple of weeks later, I returned to LA followed by Oliver and Hervé, who were about to do their next respective projects.

As to the inspiration for the film's story, Oliver had written it from a nightmare that he himself had had. I have no idea why the film was retitled to *Seizure* as thematically it had nothing to do with word.

I went back to Rome, and to Maurizio.

Soulmate - Maurizio Bonuglia

## ■ THE LAST ITALIAN TANGO

*Ultimo Tango A Zagarol*, otherwise translated as *The Last Italian Tango*, was a send up of a film that starred Marlon Brando, *Last Tango in Paris*. In my film, I played a young woman who meets a man who has just abandoned his wife, and then I drag him into a sadomasochistic relationship within an empty flat. It was a comedy that also starred a top comedian in Rome; a major star called Franco Franchi. Making this film was a lot of fun, but every now and again Franco would try it on with me. Telling him no didn't work and I had really had enough of this. One scene in the film saw him naked and in a bath. I was bathing him. He had really annoyed me so, in the middle of the scene, I put my hand in the water, 'Scuse, where is you cock, I cannot find it?' The director and the crew fell about laughing hysterically, but he was furious. But this time it worked, I had got him, he backed off, and we carried on very well after that.

In the final scene we did a tango where I finish writhing on the floor. I laugh every time I see this scene. He and I worked well together and we made a very funny film.

I was still with Maurizio, but we had started fighting, physically. Our combined fieriness was taking us in a really downward spiral. We separated and we went off with different people. We later saw each other in Piazza Navona. We stopped, said something to each other. He then slapped my face and without thinking, I slapped him back. Basically, we were both a couple of fucking drama queens.

And that, we thought, would be the last we would see of each other.

## ■ THE KISS

…Until we found ourselves filming together for *Il bachio della morte*, *The Kiss of Death*. Later becoming *Il Bacio* due to other similarly named films being in existence, it was a historical story where I played a strange dancer who dabbled in black magic and fell in love with the married Guido Rambaldi as played by Maurizio. This film had me at the most beautiful as I have ever appeared in film. The wigs were all handmade, the make-up was creative and delicate, and the clothes were tailored to perfection. The crew spent a lot of time to ensure the lighting accentuated the earlier work. I had two major dances to learn. Directed by Mario Lanfranchi, who was married to super opera star, Anna Moffo, *The Kiss* was Lanfranchi's first film. Experienced in theatre and television, with Anna, he was very responsible for bringing opera to television. Filmed on location in Venice and Rome in and amongst the cities' very beautiful buildings, the film exuded a very operatic feel. The film was really quite beautiful; stunning.

It didn't matter that Maurizio had a girlfriend and I had a lover. Those feelings for each other had not dissipated due simply because we had romantically forged ahead. His girlfriend went away; my lover was still around. In one scene I had to do a particularly erotic dance for Maurizio's character, whereby, just like the *Dance of the Seven Veils*, I wore and had to remove several veils to reveal my breasts as I performed for him. The dance had us both ending on a white bear rug. During this performance, his character was stoned on some drugs my character had previously given to him.

Just before filming the scene, we decided to actually get stoned. We were completely ripped. We did the scene, we ended up on the rug as scripted, but we couldn't stop writhing over each other. The director shouted at us and still we could not stop; no one could stop us. In the end, the director continued to shout at us until we stopped. It was hilarious.

Our connection had always been deep. Years later, he came to LA for a visit, and although we did not resume our sexual relationship, we still loved each other dearly. I introduced him to the Ranch, of which I speak more later, and Death Valley, and all the tribes fell in love with him. He was very special. I last saw him in Rome with his lovely wife, Rosanna. He died a few years ago and I still miss him dearly.

Both the films were ADR'd, looped, dubbed. I was not fluent in Italian. I understood enough for casual conversation and I was able to make people laugh and hopefully adore me, but mine was like pig Italian. I didn't have any ability to use grammar. I would just pull in the words in a certain order to make myself understood. Regarding the filming, I would say some words in English, some I said normally and without affectation. And there were some words I would have to say in Italian for the movement of my mouth and the later dubbing. The script was in both Italian and English. Many British people had moved to Rome because of the availability of work. I met the fascinatingly snaky and hilarious Vladek Sheybal on the set of *Il Bacio* for the first time, even though we had previously co-starred in *From Russia with Love*.

Rome took my breath away. I consider it to be the most beautiful city I have ever known. By this point I had also been to Paris, Munich and Amsterdam, but Rome topped them all. The beautiful piazzas, where the evening would be filled by people undertaking the ritualistic 'passeggiata', the early evening wander to facilitate the gatherings of friends for drinks and flirting. It was a time of the day for a little drink, and if you were having a drink, you would also be served cicchetti; little bits of pizza, squares of sandwiches, and teeny nibbles. The Italians are the true connoisseurs of the art of flirting! Everyone flirts. By way of comparison, England is not terribly good for flirting. In Italy, it does not mean that if you flirt, you have to fuck. If you happen to rub shoulders, it does not mean you have to marry them. A slight caress, a laugh, a look; it is like a dance and it is something I do miss. I was in my element. I flirt with my girls, with everyone. The key word for the Italians is, Fun. And particularly the Romans, they have a delicious sense of humour. Luckily, I spoke and understood enough of the language to understand them, the slightly different accents and their humour. I love the Roman sense of humour; it is not far from that of the Jamaican humour. It is slightly philosophical, but in a non-English sarcastic way, a real banter, more playful.

The language is incredibly romantic and in fact has to be the one I love to hear when making love which of course is a forte of theirs!! I wish I had learned it properly; I think I might have been a natural linguist. I was good at Spanish and Latin when I was at school in in Jamaica. But I am a lazy cow, and I was too busy having fun to go to school. I still swear in Italian having picked it all up while I was there.

I am not a pizza person, except when in Italy where they are absolutely delicious. Everything always tastes incredibly fresh. There is a simplicity and freshness to Italian food that I adored. It was the same with the pastas, of which I was introduced to so many different varieties, and to so many sauces. I preferred the simple ones, tomato based and spicy. There is one recipe that to this day I will make at home and serve it as the 'very famous' Mamma Martine's Arrabiata. The Italian sauces are not like the French ones that tend to be creamier. The Italian sauces are much cleaner and they tend not to cover the foods, more they serve to flavour them. Just delicious. I discovered Polenta; like a soft cake, it is also divine. And the meats. One of my favourite meals was fegato alla veneziana, calve's liver cooked the Venetian way; a dish which to this day I still adore.

Ice creams, the Italian ice cream is beyond beyond. And not just in Rome, but all over Italy. I found them to die for, even as a person who does not have a sweet tooth. The Italians are fiercely proud of their foods. The best 'gelateria' would be decided and there would be a line of people waiting to be served. Second best was not an option. If there is a best, there is a queue for it. I came across flavours that I never thought of. Although well-known today, it was where I discovered Pistachio. For me I find Italian food to be on a par with the Japanese Sashimi, the celebration of pure clean taste.

It would be almost redundant to say I loved the intricate fountains, the iconic buildings and their architecture. I found on entering these monuments I would literally experience a physical sensation that would connect with the history of the place. We were outside the Colosseum filming. I was aware of the Colosseum's history that saw lions released in the ring to kill and devour the Christians by way of punishment for their belief and faith. During our filming, there were hundreds of cats milling around the Colosseum; more so than anywhere else in Rome. It was almost like they were drawn to what had happened centuries before.

I was in awe of the Pantheon building. My feelings were one of excitement; I couldn't believe how many years ago it had been built. The Pantheon was my favourite. My mother came to visit me in Rome; she really only travelled to see her family and to be with them. She did not travel for the sake of travel alone.

It was great to see her. She wanted to go to St Peter's Basilica. Again, through earlier knowledge and awareness, I knew it was a building that I would find to be truly evil. Not least because they have so much money while there is so much poverty, but also because of the terrible abuse the priests inflicted upon children. To me it seemed weird. Enormous numbers of gifts had been given to the pope from around the world and they were all horded in main halls, or underneath the ground floor in store rooms, including incredible jewels that they could have used to help the poor. But no, they were hording it all. I had heard it all before. I did not want to go but, my mummy wanted to see it and so we went. It is not just a stunning building, but a city, and admittedly I was in awe. We were entering the main body of the building, the area the Pope would be with his people around him. As I entered, my whole body began to shake, it was a horrible experience. I needed some time, some space. Mummy asked if I was ok. I had a vision. I was in front of the red carpet where the Pope sat, but instead of the carpet, I was seeing blood, a wave of blood which was moving. I had to gather myself and turn away, 'It is not there, you are imagining it,' I told myself. But it was horrible. I finished the tour, but it got to me. A part of me recognised and appreciated the amazing and accomplished artistry, but something there horrified me, made me angry and upset.

It is fair to say that Rome amplified my Extra Sensory Perception. I experienced many physical manifestations when walking into buildings. I had visions, sensory experiences; all parts of the ESP trip. My ESP was high in London, but it became much higher in Rome. I believed I had been there before, perhaps with Maurizio. Both Maurizio and I felt the same; that we had been in Rome in a previous life. As life has progressed, the ESP has manifested itself much less, and I am glad it is less. It had been far too much in the past. In LA, I had friends who were channelers and healers but it was different there. A part of me goes way back to Africa, a nation whose population had a whole different head for this stuff. I believe that 'this' comes from both my Jamaican and African roots.

John had done a film with Tony Curtis before we went to California. I wasn't working so I stayed in a lovely hotel near the Spanish Steps in Piazza di Spagna. This was where and when I discovered painting. I bought a seat, an easel, and all the paints. When I go into something, I go full in so I got the full set, all the stuff. And I sat on my balcony in my bikini and I started to paint in oils. And, even though I say it myself, I am rather good. I still have the first painting I ever did.

I had also been a keeper of diaries. Even though I was leading a tearaway life, I managed to maintain very detailed accounts of what I had been up to. I had started when I was in school and as my life started taking me down different avenues, together with the naughtiness, I wrote everything down. One of the diaries had a lock on it. And now I see just why you should have locks on them! But then when I moved to Rome, I lost all my diaries. I had moved so many times that things just got left behind. When I was in Rome, I started again. However, when I fled the city, those diaries were left behind. I hope they are never found as those diaries would be telling in all sorts of ways. I hope they never reappear.

I loved Rome, and will always love Rome, but I was missing terribly a sisterhood. I had lovely male friends but had not really connected with any female friends in Rome. On *The Kiss*, I had a lover called Pierluigi Ciriaci, the film's Production Manager. He was terribly sweet and adoring, and understood my unhappiness of not having girlfriends. He offered, 'If you really want to go to LA, I will give you a ticket. But you have to leave as soon as you can. And I will take care of your flat.'

I packed one suitcase and I left for LA, leaving behind my diaries, my photographs, my everything; an entire life.

# 10

# CALIFORNIA,
# WORK / LOVE / RETIREMENT

## ◼ ARRIVAL

My good friend, casting director and agent, Robert Walker, picked me up from the airport on 9th March 1974 and he suggested I could stay with him again until I got myself sorted out. His was still in the house in Beverley Hills and I was assigned a room in the rear quarters of his property.

I was really happy to be back in LA. Whereas I had had lovers in Rome and had found work, the Roman girls were a different breed. They were almost not to be trusted. At worst, there had been a betrayal but at best, there were some older ladies with whom I had tea but generally, in Rome you are always a 'stranieri', a foreigner. You're sort of accepted, and kind of involved, but ultimately if you're not Italian, or not Roman, you will always be an outsider. And that had something to do with my leaving Italy. To this point, I had never met bitchy women, until in Rome, and I did not understand it that you could have some fun, and be invited to a party but if you were considered to be an outsider due to being a 'stranieri', it, the city of Rome, might forever be closed off to me.

I missed having girlfriends, female friends. Not necessarily the girls I had made friends with in LA or London; but just good solid female friends.

103

It was bliss to be here in LA and being with Robert was the right decision. I stayed with him for a year and a half, and as well as a friend and my agent, he became a major person in my life. As a casting director before he set himself up as an agent, he 'discovered' a lot of people as actors. His first was a Las Vegas showgirl called Valerie Perrine. As soon as he met her, he had the idea to put her in a film called *Slaughterhouse-Five*. He also represented Barbara Carrera. He saw someone on a train in LA, a guy who was working on it as a trainman, brakeman and conductor. He introduced himself and asked him if he had ever considered acting. In this way, Kevin Dobson became another person with agent representation subsequent to being 'found' by Robert. He just found these people, the younger ones.

His best friend, Monique James, was the head of contract players at Universal. She was the last person to have this role at Universal as this was a time when people were contracted to specific studios. She was a huge success. Robert would take one look at a person and have an idea. The person might have no experience, and had not even thought about acting. He would then approach Monique, she would say Yes ok, and put them under Universal contract. Robert and Monique had gone to college together. Each of the 'discovered' actors would then be offered training, and as a part of that training, they would be given small parts in films and television to give them real life experience on film sets and locations. Unfortunately, I never went under contract and nor was it on offer. I would certainly have been up for it but I think the idea of contract players was just on its way out as I arrived in LA for the second time.

A frequent visitor to Robert's house was Barbara Carrera, the Nicaraguan model turned actress. I was in awe of her; whatever she did, however she sat, she was perfect. She would only have to cross her legs and she would be gorgeous. I would just sit there, watching her; she was An Exotic. Robert put her in one of her first films, a sci-fi movie called *Embryo*. I think possibly she also stayed with us for a while. On one evening, the producer Robert Evans picked her up to take her out. Seven times married and the producer of *The Godfather, Chinatown* and *Marathon Man*, the perma tanned gentleman had by then already attained a bad boy reputation. He was somehow involved with the Mafia, and he had been implicated in the gangland style murder of Roy Radin. As he entered the house, hair swept back and wearing his trademark turtle neck sweater, I remember my body went into revolt. I had an immediate reaction of danger and bad vibes. I backed up and disappeared to another room.

Robert loved to look at houses. He bought a place in Cambria, just four hours from LA. It became another place for his tribes to gather at weekends. We called him the Baron. And we called the house Baronia. He became the Baron of Baronia.

Any time a new guest came to stay, the Baron would have a ritual to induct them into his Kingdom. Everyone would dress up in costumes from a trunk amidst a great deal of giggling. The Baron would then ask the participant to relinquish all their worldly goods. Once in a while, a guest would not get the joke, but on receiving his blessing, he would go into his jeweller in the little town and order gold medallions for the 'knightesses' and rings for the knights. I was so special, that I got a ring instead of a medallion which I still wear today.

Michael Taylor was another important person in my life upon my return to LA. Michael had lived and worked as a model in New York. Neil Dillard was Michael's lover. Neil's sister was Jennifer Dillard. At the time of my arrival, she was just 17. I was in my 30s, but we were about the same size and she was just as naughty as me. She was very bright. Robert hired her as a secretary in his agency. We all started to lock in. Gayle Taylor was Michael's sister. She too became a part of our tribe.

Jonathan Demme and his wife, Maud, were also in LA when I arrived. Many of the people who I had connected with in London in the 1970s were gathering in LA. Jonathan was getting finance and people together for his first directorial, *Caged Heat*, with Barbara Steele. Barbara had been under contract with John at Rank, in the 1950s. She was now a huge horror queen in both LA and Italy. She was huge. She and I became friends.

I hunted and gathered my friends. Later in 1998 when I was returning to live in London, my mother asked me what I was going to do about friendships. I said I would go hunting and gathering, to which she replied that I just had too many friends and it would end up in being confusing. Not to me, I said.

I started dating a producer, Larry Turman, of *The Graduate*. It hadn't been and wasn't really my thing to date producers and directors, as they would usually be a lot older than me. Born in 1926, he was 15 years my senior. He was keen, fun and recently separated from his wife. He had taken a house for the summer in the gated community, Malibu Colony. Long since known as an enclave of luxury homes, it had enticed stars from the golden age of cinema such as Barbara Stanwyck and Bing Crosby to call it home. Larry knew Larry Hagman very well. He decided to throw a party for him and 20 or so other people. I am his girlfriend. 'Can you cook,' he asks. I did a shepherd's pie for 24 people. Paul Newman and his wife also came to the party. The first time I had seen him on screen, I thought he was the most gorgeous thing I had ever seen. We met and we clicked. He was a very private man, not at all a social being. His wife, Joanne Woodward, was fabulous. Through talking to them, I felt a deep connection for their craft. They became the key to the party; they even complimented me on my pie. While Larry was not my true love, he was very kind and he introduced me to a lot people. We both knew it wouldn't last long, but while it did last, we both had a nice time.

I had some friends around me, I had a lover. Now it was time to get back to work. My first part was for an episode of *The Wide World of Mystery* TV series. Running from 1973 to 1978, it was an anthology series of mystery, horror and suspense stories. Each episode lasted for 90 minutes and it was a form of live TV, whereby one would rehearse for a few days and then perform it as a piece of theatre. Some episodes were taped to video, others were not, which led to some episodes being forever 'lost'.

My episode was called *Stand by for Murder*. I Played Linda, the wife of a TV executive who thinks she might have committed a murder, and if that question were not enough to provide upset, is tormented by a stalker inside an empty TV station. Shirley Knight was the star and the director; she was terrific. It was my entry back into work but I wasn't jumping for joy; it was not a great piece of television. While the production might have been live, it was not in front of an all-important audience. I had done a little bit of theatre in Rome, an Agatha Christie piece with the daughter of Tyrone Power in a gorgeous little theatre. In this play, I had taken the role of an American movie star. We were all very scared. It had been my first real theatre piece and I was ready to throw up through the whole production. So too actually were the other actors, even if they were by then used to theatre. The production lasted just a week. On one occasion, Burt Lancaster showed up and I began to really get my knickers in a twist. He was one of my favourite actors. He was in Rome to win over Federico Fellini's heart about a film called *La Strada*. Even though he was Dino De Laurentis' first choice, Fellini went with Anthony Quinn to play the role of Zampanò. Would Burt at least enjoy the theatrical play? There were only 20-30 people in audience. Burt sat right in front of me and I had understood that my dress was slightly 'see through'. The play started and our eyes met, he smiled with all his teeth, I saw his smile and I almost faltered. But I came back. My heart was pounding. At the end we all took a bow, and he applauded us. I thought he must be applauding just me. I wanted to jump off the stage and into his arms. It made my foray into theatre a wonderful experience, but it also demonstrated the actors' need for an audience for a live production. Needless to say, the *Stand by for Murder* episode was not the same thing, nor was it the most exciting part of my life.

## ◼ STRANGE NEW WORLD

In October 1975 I did *Strange New World*, a TV film that was a loose trilogy from the stable of Gene Roddenberry and starred John Saxon. It was an interesting sci-fi film where I played Tana, a part of a medical team that has survived a state of long-term hibernation, or suspended animation in space only to come back to an apocalyptic Earth. John Saxon played Captain Anthony Vico and James Olson played a surgeon as a sort of Dr. Frankenstein of the film. The writer producer was Ronald Graham, a friend who continued in my life as a supporter and a promoter.

I found the premise interesting because the people the three survivors of the space lab meet on earth are a group of immortals called the Eternans, who have lost the ability to reproduce and have survived by cloning themselves and harvesting their clones for replacement body parts. The surgeon, as played by Jim Olson, is a 200-year-old former medical student of one of the three space lab survivors and who is now suffering from the onset of dementia. However, the cloning has cost the Eternans their natural immunity; they only survive thanks to a decontamination field that keeps germs out, and the hope to incorporate the immunity factors of the three survivors' un-cloned blood into the Eternans' genes.

This film was the first sci-fi I had done, and it made me think about cloning, and how it might happen for real. As an actor, Jim was so strange that he made it interesting. He gave the whole film a bizarre feel to it. And in fact, to the shoot. It really was a strange new world. He made me feel like we were in it. It made it exciting, and very atmospheric. As a result, I came into work with the excitement of having created that aura. It was a very interesting 8-10 days' work.

Robert Walker was a friend of George Nader, a discreetly gay leading actor of both film and television. Both George and his life partner, Mark Miller, were long term and very close friends with Rock Hudson. George had invited Robert to join him and Mark for a birthday party at Rock's home in the hills above Mulholland Drive in the Santa Monica Mountains. The party was for Rock Hudson.

The entertainment world was possibly aware that Rock Hudson was gay, but it was never openly discussed, as it was not really accepted. When we arrived, the party was in full swing all around the pool. I met Rock and he was lovely, and quite the flirtiest of men. It was lovely to have had that moment with him. He really was a very handsome man. Some of my boys had by then already been to his house for parties and they had told me he was gay. And then of course there were the rumours that were always threatened to be confirmed in the magazine, Confidential, which would signal the immediate downfall of the actors whose proclivities went that way. There were many gay superstars, but it was kept undercover. I went with my boys to one other party at Rock's.

## ■ ERHARD SEMINAR TRAININGS

I had not found my way back into the LA Hollywood working scene. I was living with my agent, Robert Walker. Many things were happening, and there were many new movements. Of which one was the newly created Erhard Seminars Training. Michael had discovered this, had participated in it and recommended it to me. What exactly was this? Whether this was how it was advertised at the time, today's recording of the courses inform that the critical part of the training was to free oneself from the past, to explore one's recurrent patterns and problems and, as a result of engaging with the course, to thereby choose to change them for the better. The course enabled one to bring into full awareness the repetition of old, burdensome behaviours and the seminars sought to enable participants to shift the state of mind around which their lives were organized. To attempt to get satisfaction or to survive from the changes, and to experience and enable in the present moment

The person behind this thinking and purporting thereof was a man called Werner Erhard, an American author and lecturer. The thinking and the courses were at the time gaining traction and notoriety. Engaging with the course meant committing to two weekends and a mid-week meeting. The weekend; Saturday commenced at 8.00am and finished on Sunday anywhere between 2.00am and 4.00am. It was the same on Sunday. There were 250 people all locked in a room, a hotel conference room. Breaks were minimal. Going to the bathroom was not possible outside whatever breaks had already been organised. Food was offered at the beginning of the day. The purpose behind this structure was to break down all the bullshit that we were carrying around with us. It was a big deal in the 1970s. It was, I think, a journey one had to take. Especially as an actor if you were trying to find the essence and the foundation to what you wanted to bring to the production.

Day 1, the trainer who will lead us through the process stood with chalk in hand in front of a blackboard and began with a quote from Plato. 'The unexamined life is not worth living.' So, this was all about examining how we lived our lives, our belief systems, our honesty, and our authenticity. The training was committed to opening the space for us to look at our bullshit. An often-used word. In order to change the patterns we lived by and to arrive at a real level of authenticity. After several hours, the trainer invited us to share our thoughts and feelings with the 249 other people in the room. A scary thought. At this point, volunteer assistants produced microphones to anyone who was willing to share. I stepped up immediately, of course. I wanted to get right in and I surprised myself with my first share.

I said, 'I realise I borrow money. But it takes me a long time to pay it back.' I was immediately embarrassed by this admittance, even though I was here and ready to open up myself up and to admit the shit. The trainers would listen, they would not judge. However, the trainer came right up to me and faced me with many questions, which made me even more embarrassed of my admittance.

What was the story behind my admittances? It, the problem, had clearly started while I was in the UK and Rome. But here in LA, I had had a bit of money to buy a car and food. I hadn't been working, I borrowed money but I was not very reliable in paying it back. Indeed, not in the slightest bit reliable. I always had an excuse, and all the excuses were ridiculous. And it was while I was in the training that I immediately saw how I was living my life. I was just not honest, even though to this point I had been thinking that I had been honest. But now I saw myself as being not in the slightest bit authentic. It pierced my heart, and I was also angry because I saw all the excuses for who I had then been. It was incredibly dramatic, and I loved the drama for the sake of the drama, but this drama, unlike that which might have been created on a movie set or in a party, made me hate what I then saw in myself.

And the few days continued in this vein. People would find themselves laughing, or crying, or falling asleep, and then someone would wake you up. On the one hand you heard stories from others that resonated exactly with how you had been behaving, but then you would get pissed off at them - even though it might have been exactly how you yourself had been behaving. It was all very much like the military training you saw in the movies, or presumably what the actual military recruits would be submitted to. Although in the military, that process was to instil in the soldiers how they should listen, respond to instruction and stand in formation. Either way, we were to be toughened up. 'Break us down and build us up', from a foundation of honesty.

Even if any of the 250 people thought they were good at whatever it was that they did in life, very quickly they realised in fact that they were not.

We left at 4am, went home, flopped into bed, and we were back at 8am on the Sunday. Lack of sleep is now playing a part of the experience; it made one more vulnerable. No sleep, no food. Food came only in the morning, and no more. It was likened to that of a Nazi camp.

It was the last weekend and everyone's nerve endings were raw. I wanted to share, I found one moment, I stood up; the room could feel the energy. I said, 'I am going to share. I.......' And then I was hysterical. Whatever it was I was going to say, it had gone. The trainer came to me. 'Where are you? How old are you?' he asks.

'I am six!' I had gone back to being six, and doing poetry in front of people. I had a nice voice, I was a pretty girl, I had a poem, and as I opened my mouth to recite it, I couldn't remember a word of it. I was in fear. Perhaps it was connected to the acting, I can't remember, I couldn't remember, so I went back to being six years old. I was devastated, it was so real. And my trainer, he just stood there. 'I am 6 and I can't remember,' I finished.

The reality hit me in writing these words as hard as it had hit me then. The tears were streaming down my face. Ugly crying in front of 249 people. It was devastating and enlightening.

Back in the seminar, it had hit the whole room; a bomb had gone off. People started to pick into things within themselves, they had started crying. There was a room-wide vulnerability, we were tight, we were all facing so much of ourselves. I had broken a wall at that point and had opened a fucking floodgate. I was drained. But it somehow had made me feel lighter. It was the end of the fourth day. It had been a big big moment for me, and for the whole room. When the seminar had ended, we all felt like we had known each other so intimately, we had uncovered all of our shit in front of each, there was a lot of hugging. People said, 'I am glad you helped me. It had been truly cathartic; it afforded a new mind set. I had not expected that. I believe none of us had.

Had this been a temporary blip from which you would fall back into the old ways? Part of the course had been to instruct, 'Well, now how are you going to come to terms with all this?' From that point henceforth I have been living in a different way, I have been seeing things differently, for the better, more organised, more structured, more respectful. I have been looking at life from a different point of view. Firstly, to have accepted who I am, but to have then started to make proper commitments to myself and to the world.

I followed this up with many other seminars. I think around 10 or so, one every following week. I found it to be a form of psychiatry; to deal with the mind in a heavy weight fashion, but with a hammer.

Then the reality hit. I had to apologise to all the people to whom I had been dishonest. This was regarding the borrowing of money and the presentation of my values. I was really sorry. Together with the borrowing of money, I always used to be late. Not just 2 to 5 mins, or an hour late; maybe I just never turned up. I was not there, present. That was awful to discover how disrespectful and shitty I had been. Time and Money mean many things to many people, and I had been walking all over that. The seminar opened up a path to owning up to my behaviour. Previously to all this, I had thought I was 'lovely' and 'grand' and 'brilliant'. Far from it. The most awful part of the course was in the discovering of yourself, to look through a window and to see only a black hole. Thank God for the course then.

Any time I might have been falling back to the old and bad habits, the tribe, and Michael would only have to say, 'Martine.' 'Yes,' I would reply. 'I know, got it.' We would each pull the other up; it made us love each other even more.

## ROY'S RESTAURANT

My acting 'star' was still yet to be catapulted into its ascendency. Money was tight and I fell into a form of work that is an actor's rite of passage. I was at a party in August 1976 in Malibu. I met a number of people, one of whom was Roy Silver who at the time was a personal manager to Bob Dylan, Bill Cosby, Joan Rivers, Richard Pryor and other similarly big names. Roy also loved to cook; I mean Really loved to cook; so much so that he set aside one day a week whereby he would work for that day in a restaurant kitchen in the Valley. And he would vary the restaurants in which he cooked. There came a point when the enjoyment in cooking outweighed that of personally managing and he stopped the latter to concentrate on the former. In 1976, at the age of 45, and together with his business partner, Ron Kreitzman, he opened a restaurant on Sunset Boulevard to cook his Chinese fusion food favourites. He called it Roy's.

When I met him, he immediately said, 'I know who you are.' He told me his story and that he had just opened this restaurant. He asked me, 'How are you doing, how's work in acting? If you are looking for some between money, come and see me. Maybe you could be our hostess.' I later saw him, we had dinner and drinks but by this time, he had someone as a hostess, an ex-ballet dancer called Frances Davis; herself an ex of a jazz musician Miles Davis. 'Look', I said, 'I could do some waitressing for you.' 'Are you sure? You do have a career.' Truth be told, I Had a career but finding it again was a work in progress; work was for me thin on the ground at this point.

With no prior experience, I began waitressing. It was a big learning curve but Roy was very clever. He hired only actors, dancers and artists as waitresses, all personalities who had found themselves out of work. He also hired Cathy, a real waitress out of New York to train us. A professional waitress, she cracked the whip, she was very good at the job. We would have weekly meetings with her to find out what we had been doing right and wrong. The food was delicious; the place he had created was a wonderful set up. There were booths, the lighting was low, the bar had the best of every form of alcohol; it had all the spirits. And Roy taught his chefs all his favourite recipes.

I decide to get my girls involved. I also had Sally, Gayle and Jennifer hired as waitresses; I had my gang with me, all amazing characters. The uniform was a geisha type of creation that wrapped around you but had pockets for money and 'other things'. There were no menus, we had playing cards each of which described a different dish. We had a stack of cards for the whole range. We handed the cards to the customers, and then we got their drinks; it was all very grand. To order from us, very simply, the customers passed back to us the cards that described what they wanted for dinner. Brilliant, we didn't have to write anything down except perhaps if multiple people chose the same dish. The plates and bowls were fabricated from very heavy Chinese porcelain, and the serving trays were Huge. The presentation started to become theatrical, probably due to the staff's background. We brought out a standing tray rest in one hand; we would throw it into position, and land the tray heaving with the Asian foods from the other hand. 'Here you are!' It was all very exciting, and the whole restaurant became something truly amazing, very much a top and IN venue to which every star came. One of the booths came with a curtain so when the really big stars came in, we could close the curtain from excited eyes. Donna Summer was a regular, as she was already good friends with Roy. In the end, we found we had different favourite tables for different people, those people might also have had a favourite waitress, all of which could be asked for.

However, this was a time where there were a lot drugs. Everyone was on everything, including the waitresses, chefs, owners, and the clientele; it was non-stop. The pockets mentioned above that also held 'other things', these were those other things. The waitresses would get to their table and we would have to pretend we were properly 'together'. But so then did the guests have to pretend they too were on form. It was all very lively and fun; quite unique really.

Someone related to President Jimmy Carter, either personally or professionally, once came to the restaurant with all his be-suited FBI agents. The agents first cased the joint before permitting the VIP to enter. What was going on? We were hysterical. In the middle of the same evening, the Stevie Wonder song, *Isn't She Lovely*, was played and Frances performed a whole dance down the centre of the restaurant. Everyone always waited in anticipation for this moment. She had been a proper dancer, there was much applause. She would take a theatrical bow before going back to being a 'hostess'. Another occasion saw a huge party come in, and all the girls disappeared. A bunch of people from the NAACP, The National Association for the Advancement of Coloured People had come in, 10 of them. I ended up taking the table because they were known to be a feisty lot. So, I was a little scared. I greeted the table with my best Jamaican accent which immediately, thank God, broke the ice and we all ended up in having a very good evening.

There was another huge party at the restaurant that had invited every star in the business, including Marlon Brando. 'Oh my God. Marlon's here'. But I knew him; I had previously met him in London as he was at the time dating my friend, Esther Anderson and, when I came to LA with John, we were in touch and had been invited to his house for an evening. Everyone is in a right royal state of star power panic. He was stood at the door; we saw each other, I walked up to him and gave him a big hug. He had an extraordinary charisma and I wish I had known him longer. He didn't come out a lot; it was unusual to see him in public.

Roy's bartender was Buddy Micucci. His sister, Mary, would bring in to Roy's a wonderful dessert called a Mandarin Orange Roll. Initially an air stewardess, she became the top caterer in LA starting her own company, Along Came Mary. She did the Emmys, the Grammys, and various Premieres. I worked with her on a Grammy event for 4000 people where she would have to know how many vegetarians, pescatarians, carnivores there were and she delivered. She ran it like a military operation checking every plate as it came out, and it blew my mind at the quality of her food and service.

I loved Roy. He was an odd character, Jewish, not exactly gorgeous but he had a lovely personality. And he treated his waitresses very well. If ever there was a time when we would mention that 'Table 7 hasn't put a tip down,' he would add it to the next tab.

I worked there 3-4 days a week for a year. It was good money too. Sometimes you could make a $100 tip off one table. And maybe because of everything else the guests had been imbibing, they wouldn't eat the food either, so we would have dinner catered to as well. We all made money, we all had a good time. There have been various attempts to write a book about this restaurant but, since it was so 'of its time' and the fact that so many names would have to be mentioned to provide context, it has never been written. And rightly so I think. When the restaurant closed, Roy and Ron organised a reunion party in a wonderful old Chinese restaurant on Vine Street in Hollywood, and we all shared outrageous and hilarious stories about our times together.

The life however began to take its toll. The nights were late, the days were long. I looked at myself in the mirror; my face was hanging off and I was beginning to look a little stretched and old.

Aspen saved me.

## ■ DOUG HAYES

Doug Hayes was a director who was well-known for the films, *Maverick*, *Ice Station Zebra* and a variety of mini-series on US television. We had worked together in LA on a few productions and we liked each other. For a brief time, he became one of my champions; he was always thrilled when he got me in to one of his productions. The first time we worked together was in 1976 on an episode of *City of Angels*, a weekly adventure series following the exploits of a hard-boiled 1930s detective, Jake Axminster and starring Wayne Rogers, Elaine Joyce and Clifton James.

Doug then wrote a part for me in the 1976 television series, *Captains and Kings*. He even wrote the character's name to be Martinique and who had my island background, my spirituality and whatever quality he saw in me that resonated with him. In the end, as the part was so well written, first Joan Collins wanted it and then Barbara Parkins. He could not pull it off. He couldn't swing it with the studio or the network. He kept on trying; he didn't stop. But the part went to Parkins. It was such a good part and I was pissed when it disappeared from my radar. 'Next time,' he said, 'I will write not such a great part, nor too huge, and it will be yours.

And in 1977, he did exactly that with *Aspen* and, as above, at exactly the right time.

*Aspen* was a three-part TV series about the trial of an Aspen man who had been accused of the rape and murder of a teenager. It starred Sam Elliott, Perry King and Gene Barry. My involvement in *Aspen* was an apology for the fact that I couldn't do *Captains and Kings*. Of the three episodes, I did two. The part I prophetically played turned out to be that of a coke addict.

Coke was rampant in LA at the time. If you went to a party, there would likely be as much coke on offer as drink. I did some research, some non-participatory research. I called a lot of people and yes, one could die from an overdose of a heart attack. This was not as well-known back then as today so I went back to all my coke fiends and said, 'So, I have found out this…' and informed them as to all I had learned.

One of my coke-infused scenes was with the actor, Anthony Franciosa. I had met Tony before but it was our first scene where we were communally high. We decided to have a puff in our trailers just prior to filming the scene. It was a stupid idea. Of course, we thought it was a fabulous idea; we would lend authenticity. But we couldn't remember the words. We started panicking. What were we going to do? We would just have to do it; we were bad children and undoubtedly, we would have to pay for it. We got on to the set and we did manage to do the scene, but I swore I would never do that again. We had had the best intentions but it opened our eyes. When I was in Rome, I had done the exact same thing before, but that was for a scene that involved dancing and collapsing on a white rug with an ex-lover. This scene had required dialogue.

The cast was terrific and Sam Elliott was a lovely man. I was very happy. Doug later looked after me again by casting me in the 1979, *The French Atlantic Affair* with a lot of people, including Telly Savalas, Louis Jourdan, Richard Jordan and Donald Pleasance. I played Donald's character's wife for a day or two's work.

The coincidental timing of moving from Roy's to Aspen was also when I went into a periodic bout of self-cleansing. The excesses of the 1970s LA scene had to be excised. I would cut myself off from men, excess food, drugs, drinking and smoking. Taking one to two months, I would fast for 11 days. It was important. It had served my balance when my eyes were opened after I had OD'd in Jamaica. I would continue to partake in all the above, but after a period, I would know the moment when I needed to effect a balance. Roy's no longer existed. It was always going to be an environment where burn out would be quick. Opening in 1977, it closed in the early 1980s. A venue called House of Blues took over the spot. I briefly saw Roy again after I had left his restaurant. He wasn't well; he had a brain tumour that was to take his life in 2003.

## ■ THE SIX MILLION DOLLAR MAN

*The Six Million Dollar Man* was a science fiction stroke action television series that starred Lee Majors as a former astronaut, Steve Austin. Austin, the astronaut, was subjected to an accident that left him near death, but NASA decided to rebuild him with bionic implants which gave him ridiculous strength, speed and vision. Having spent all that money, NASA then handed him over to be controlled and operated by the Office of Strategic Operations, or the 'OSO', to be a quasi-secret agent. It was perfect 1970s space age television, but that which was based on a 1972 novel called *Cyborg,* by Martin Caidin.

The series ran from 1973 to 1978 with each season, excepting season 1, contributing a little over 20 episodes per season. I was recruited to star in two episodes.

My first episode was in the series' second year of 1975; it happened to be the better episode of the two. Called *Outrage in Balinderry,* it was about revolutionaries who kidnap the wife of the US Ambassador to the nation of Balinderry. A character called Julia Flood was the liaison with the kidnappers, Steve Austin hooked up with her and together they attempt to free the captured wife. I was Julia Flood.

To that point, Lee Majors and I had never met. Our first day of filming, it was 8am, and of course we were instructed to have a love scene in a car. We had just stepped out of make-up, and at eight in the morning we are in love, and we kissed. Aside from the 1970s television drama, and the early morning inaugural scene, it was a really interesting part and it was great to work on. When I did the audition, I met only the producers and director, no one else. At the point of filming, it was almost laughable, 'We had just better get on with,' we said to each other. We were both prepared for it, our breaths were fresh for a kiss. Again, it was episodic TV,

116

which led to about a week's work. We filmed on the back lot of Universal Studios, together with a bit of location work in the hills. And that episode afforded some instruction on how to shoot a gun, a revolver.

My second episode was in 1976, and was called *The Thunderbird Connection*. Steve Austin was instructed to go undercover as a Thunderbird pilot to infiltrate a middle-eastern country, find a young middle-eastern prince and to smuggle him out of the country. I was in charge of said prince in said region and became Steve's liaison.

## ◼ DEATH VALLEY

In 1976, I found my own apartment and moved out of Robert's house. I shared it with an Italian woman who had just split up from her husband. It didn't last long. She was fun, lovely, but hard work. Six months later, I moved to Sycamore Avenue, just north of Hancock Park in the Wilshire area. Hancock Park had been the Beverley Hills of the old Hollywood. A lot of the stars had lived there. Developed in the 1920s, there are a lot of architecturally distinctive and Spanish looking buildings with big rooms within. One could find everything from apartments to mansions. I loved it; one could walk around the area unlike much of the rest of LA which remains un-walkable. I found the apartment and area because one of my boys had taken an apartment further down the road. They knew what had come up and they let me know. Sycamore Avenue became a really fabulous street to live on.

Three guys helped me move in; Jonathan Demme, Gary Goetzman and Joe Viola, the director of Demme's first film, *Angels Hard as They Come*. These were three guys who were readying to be big stars. They rented a van and moved me into my new flat. And my payment? I stood by the window and flashed my boobs for them. They so appreciated it.

This was also the time of the beginning of my love affair with Death Valley, the national park on the California Nevada border that has attracted the superlatives, the driest, the hottest, the lowest and the largest of all the US national parks. In 1977, my darling Michael Taylor had just seen the 1970 film *Zabriskie Point*. As well as being the name of the film, it was also the name of a part of the Amargosa Range of mountains in the eastern part of Death Valley. Michael fell in love with the place. He said he and I should visit.

117

'Oh, but darling it's a desert; there are spiders, and sand,' I said. 'Get in the car, we are going.' And we did, and it would be a part of the world I would visit three times a year while I was still in LA. Through naivety or stupidity, we didn't take food or water for our inaugural trip. But it was magical, the sand, the mountains, the dunes, the salt flats; Zabriskie Point is really a most stunning place. Luckily in the national park, we found a couple of hotels and an inn, maybe a couple of food markets. Not only did we buy food and water, we bought hiking boots. We had figured out how to do it. We then invited with us on future trips only people who we believed would or could appreciate the environment. It didn't always work; one woman I took refused to get out of the car, so enormous did she find the place.

Because parts of the park are below sea level, there were times we were at the top of a mountain and experience a snow storm. One hour to get to the bottom, it was sunny and warm. March to May, and October to November were the best times to visit from a temperance point of view, but I have also spent Xmas, New Year and Easter there. You couldn't visit in summer, as you could fry an egg on yourself in the 50-degree centigrade heats.

I was addicted to the place. It was only four hours out of LA, and with the millions of colours, the magic often drew me to it. Unless you have really experienced it, it is hard to describe. All the people I took, returned and loved it; even the girl who initially didn't get out of the car. The hours of hiking, the views, the wildlife, the birds, the sunsets, were truly magical.

Death Valley was our playground, and allowed us to be free with the help of our favourite drugs. Acid and mushrooms were provided by our trusted drug master, Michael, who always managed to find the purest of these drugs. The wild child in us all was free to indulge in the joys of this glorious desert. I danced naked in crystal sunbeams, sang in places where my voice reverberated against the rock formations, drummed and chanted to a point of utter ecstasy, watched entire sunsets and entire moon rises, and laid in the light of the moon on the sun-kissed earth. We filled our souls with divine energy to return to life in the city, renewed and revitalised.

It also gives one the odd story. Born in 1872, Walter Scott was the source of an amazing tale. Having travelled with the Buffalo Bill Cody's Wild West Show as a stunt rider for 12 years, he and his wife moved to Colorado where he tried to start a gold mine. That having failed, he conned a New York business man into

Death Valley, surveying the vis

The joy of Bad Water in Death Valley

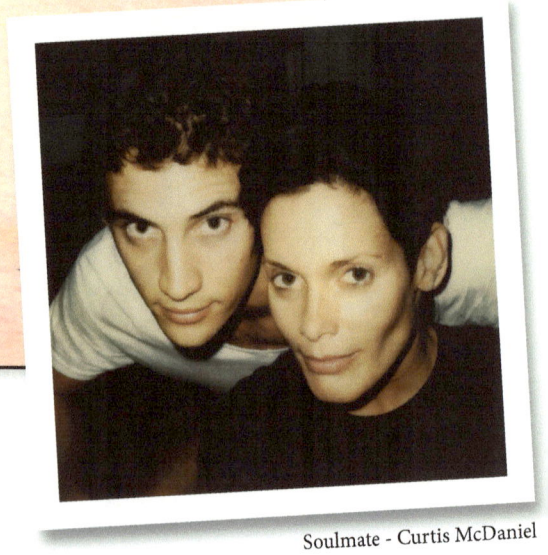
Soulmate - Curtis McDaniel

120

investing in an entirely fictitious mine. Lasting two years with having absolutely no gold to show for the investments, the investor leaves. Scott merely starts again but this time with Albert Johnson, a Chicago businessman. Johnson sunk $4000 into the scam over just a few months and then pulled out. Scott was later arrested after other investors had been shaken down, but although in trial he had been found to be a fraud, the charges were dismissed on a technicality.

For reasons best known only to Albert Johnson, he decided to visit Walter Scott in Death Valley, whereupon Johnson forgave Scott for his wayward ways, and then they became friends. Apparently just prior to this, Johnson had been quite ill, but the Death Valley air did much to improve his health, so he stayed to build a new ranch as his vacation home. Of course, Scotty, as he was by then known, declared that Johnson was building a castle for him. Resigning himself to Scotty's personality, Johnson did nothing to discourage this and the ranch became known as Scotty's Castle, even though the name at the door reads, Death Valley Ranch, and even though the 'castle' was never finished, and even though Scotty himself lived in another cabin in Lower Vine Ranch.

I found I was obsessed with this story. This character had got away with so much, he was such a conman and an incredible character that I wished someone had his story brought to life. It was so unique; not the fact that he was a conman but that he had made friends with one of the people he had conned. For years I had wanted to make a film of this story and I wrote a 10-to-15-page outline for it in the 1980s. Wanting the likes of Tom Hanks to play Scotty, I tested it with my friend, Gary Goetzmann. Unfortunately, it wasn't for him, so who knows if it will ever be made.

Marta Becket was another Death Valley story. A New York based ballerina, she had performed at the Radio City Music Hall and on Broadway. Creating a one-woman show, she took it on tour when providence dictated that she and her husband, who were driving across country, had a flat tyre in Death Valley Junction. At the junction was a small theatre built as part of a Mexican Colonial style complex that also included a hotel, offices and a store. Evidently feeling tied to nowhere, she and her husband decided to stay in Death Valley, Becket rented the theatre, repaired it and renamed it the Amargosa Opera House. Becket was also a painter and painted an entire audience in the auditorium so that whenever she performed, even if there was no one there, she would always have an 'audience'. It was in 1970 that National Geographic discovered her giving one of those performances and wrote a profile on her, which led to one of those, 'build it and they will come' moments. Visitors poured in from around the world.

With Michael, I went to see her in 1978. She was a brilliant woman, so passionate about life. We got to meet her and I am so glad we did. She was in her 60s and still performing ballet, and it was only in her later years after that, that she instead performed *The Sitting Down Show,* where - as the name suggests - she would sit and talk to her audience. I believe her last performance was in 2012. She died in her home in Death Valley Junction in 2017.

For my 39th birthday, I decided to go to Death Valley on my own. I had never visited alone before. At night it can be so dark sometimes, you could get out of the car, walk a foot away, and panic because you couldn't see the car. It was so exciting. But then equally, there were times when there were so many stars, everything was cast in an eerie but exquisite light. It was September and I had decided to spend a few days there; it was still too hot. I drove Michael's Audi and popped into a Furnace Creek gas station. I said to the strikingly handsome young man, 'I think there is a problem with the car, but I don't want any bad news.' We talked; I told him I was here for my birthday. He looked at the engine and told me that it would be all right. I left and went into Furnace Creek Diner, and a few minutes later the young man bounded in, sat down and said, 'I want to buy you a birthday breakfast.'

He really was very beautiful; he was just 19. We fell in love, and arranged a date that evening at Zabriskie Point. We took a picnic. He was a musician; he had brought his guitar with him and he played to me. This developed into a relationship that continued, on and off, for a few years. I would arrive at Furnace Creek, meet him, have an incredible affair, and then leave. And I wouldn't see him again for three months. I told Michael about him, we went to Furnace Creek to find him, he was again sitting outside his room, I leapt out of the car, and into each other's arms. His name was Curtis James McDaniel and we loved each other even though he was 20 years my junior. He was a wild child, very spiritual, and a country boy who couldn't exist in a city… And I could not live full time in Death Valley.

We were madly in love. We were like two snakes when we made love, wrapping our skins together as one. Every touch of our bodies was the most sensual experience I have ever had in my life. We spent hours just kissing, it was truly deep and beautiful.

I met his parents who of course were only a few years older than me. I looked exactly like his grandmother. She must have been one of those connections from a past life. Curtis and I separated several times. But there was a time when finally, we knew we were not going to see each other ever again. There was nothing specific in the air, there was no tension or atmosphere, we still loved each other, but as he couldn't deal with the city, we just knew this was to be the final time we would see each other. The city broke him and devoured him. He needed the trees, the air and the nature. He could have been a fabulous model. Everyone who met him loved him. And to this day, we cannot find him. He was my third soulmate, Michael, Maurizio, and Curtis. A beautiful passionate relationship where he would naturally tell me, 'Last night I danced and danced. I leapt on a moon beam and I danced for you.'

When I had come back to London, to celebrate my 60th birthday I sent an invitation to a number of my friends to meet at Zabriskie Point at sunset and on 26th September 2001, my actual birthday. A ranger turned up just when we had all taken mushrooms and told us that we could only be there for a short while. For some magical reason, when he was told it was my birthday, and we would only be there for a short while, he left us alone, even though we had illegally removed barriers to get the car and the provisions to the top of Zabriskie. The great spirit was definitely with us!

Ten friends had arrived at sunset, right on time. Because of the heat, we wore sarongs until the dancing started and the mushrooms were eaten. And then the sarongs came off. It was a beautiful night that we took all the way through to 4am. We had watched the sun set and we watched the moon rise. It was the last time I was in my beloved Death Valley.

## ■ BARETTA

*Baretta* was another US detective series that ran from 1973 to 1978. Anthony Vincenzo 'Tony' Baretta was played by Robert Blake; a terrific actor who was later accused of murdering his wife, in 2001. The episode I worked on was called *Lyman P. Dokker, Fed*. It told the story of Baretta teaming up with an FBI computer expert to retrieve stolen emeralds belonging to a sheik and, if that was not enough, they also solve the murder of a prince who was involved with a deceiving belly dancer. Of course, I was that belly dancer, and it was she who had stolen the emerald. The creativity aside, it turned out to be very intense, and it was great to work with Blake; I liked working with him.

I had to learn belly dancing through Roland Dupree and his dance academy. I had by then already taken some dance classes with Roland but not belly dancing. And it was not easy. I did not have a belly to shake about and whatever I had, had to be moved in an entirely different way. I did enjoy doing it.

And the stolen emerald, I had it secreted in my belly button.

## ◼ HART TO HART

It was great to be on this show as I had met Robert Wagner two or three times before, but I was meeting Stephanie Powers for the first time. On this show it felt like I had come home to a friend. *Hart to Hart* was a TV series that had the independently wealthy married couple, the Harts, getting caught up in all sorts of issues that required them to act first as detectives and secondly as business people. The series ran from 1979 to 1984 and I was brought in for an episode called *Murder is a Man's Best Friend*.

Playing on the phrase, 'a dog is a man's best friend', my cohort, Kenneth Mars, a comedian, take our evil frustration out on the Harts' dog, Freeway, a Löwchen or, Little Lion Dog. In our roles, we were making a new dog food and Freeway was to star in a commercial to advertise it. But for reasons best left forgotten, we wanted to hide a secret ingredient and the best way to do that was to kill the dog. We kidnapped Freeway and were evil in so many other ways that as punishment, we ended up in a big vat full of dog food. Whatever this stuff was made from, chopped up foam and goo, it got into our ears and noses, and we had to go for medical attention to have it all fished out.

Robert was a joy to work with, and the creator of the show, Tom Mankiewicz, also directed my episode. His brother, Christopher, was my best friend in Rome.

## ◼ MELVIN & HOWARD

Melvin & Howard was the first of a couple of films I did that were based on real life events. It tells the story of when Howard Hughes crashed his motorcycle in the Nevada desert and was found lying on Highway 95 by Melvin Dummar, a gas station owner. Not knowing it was 'the' Howard Hughes that he had rescued, Melvin was going to take the man to a hospital, but instead is persuaded by Hughes to take him to Las Vegas instead. Much of the rest of the film then concentrates on Melvin's erratic life until at the end of the film, a man deposits a last will and testament of Howard Hughes on the counter of his gas station.

The film was made in 1979 and was directed by my friend, Jonathan Demme, one of my protectors who was always looking to see if he could use his actor friends. His films were very American and so I did not naturally fit in but here, I had to play a fictional realtor, an estate agent. I was a con artist trying to take advantage of Melvin and his situation. He was looking for somewhere to live, and he came to me. I realised they had money, and I was looking to shake them down.

Jason Robards played Hughes and Mary Steenburgen played Melvin's first wife. She won an Oscar for this role.

## THE HAPPY HOOKER GOES HOLLYWOOD

In 1971, a prostitute called Xavier Hollander published a memoir called *The Happy Hooker: My Own Story.* Selling 20 million copies, the memoir spawned three films; *The Happy Hooker* with Lynn Redgrave, *The Happy Hooker Goes to Washington* with Joey Heatherton, and in 1980, my film, *The Happy Hooker Goes to Hollywood,* where I played the lady in question.

he *Happy Hooker Goes to Hollywood* was the first time I had my name above the titles. In Hollywood, this is a big deal. The film, by now loosely based on the memoirs, starred *Batman*'s Adam West and comedian, Phil Silvers and Jack Lemmon's son, Chris, and comedic actor, Richard Deacon. It followed a story of the Dutch prostitute heading to Hollywood and dealing with a series of crooked film producers in an attempt to get her memoirs filmed. The script was cute; it was funny. My agent, Robert, put me up for the role, I auditioned and the impression I got was that I walked away with it. The one minor question I had in my mind was that, even though I was not quite yet 40, was undressing at that age going to be ok? I thought about it; I decided I would do it. The Costume Designer, Lennie Barin, was fabulous. He designed for me the wildest outfits in jersey fabrics where underneath, I did not wear a bra and through which you could see my body. It was fine. My body was still perky, I had not gone south and the figure-hugging fabrics accentuated the perkiness.

I never got to meet Xavier Hollander; I would have loved to. In our film, Xavier is looking to make a film with a studio and the studio producer screws her over. She gets back at them by shooting her own film. The studio producer in question was played by Adam West. Adam had a dry sense of humour, and it played out in our love scenes. We were in bed, dressed, but barely so. I was on top of him and he said, 'Don't move.' 'But Adam, we have to move.' 'But what are my Batman fans going to think?' 'And my Bond fans...?'

He was lovely to work with. Indeed, everyone was lovely to work with. Except the producers.

The film was produced by The Cannon Group, and the two producers were Israeli cousins, Menahem Golan and Yoram Globus who in 1979 had taken over the ailing company. Already by the time of our film, the company and the producers had garnered a bad reputation in Hollywood. Much later, there was a documentary that delved into their professionalism and as part of the show, I was interviewed. They were dreadful.

We were towards the end of the shoot and there was a scene that required a night shoot for a pool party. Naked people were required to be in pool. One of the First Assistant Directors came to me before we were about to shoot and said to me, 'Come out and have a look at this.' The two producers had decided to descend on the location and had taken over the directing reigns. They had all the extras screwing in the pool. It was about to be a porn movie. I was so angry; they were debasing the extras and the film. What the hell were they thinking?

I yelled, 'If you don't stop this right now, I will kick this camera into the pool.' Somehow, they did stop the goings on, but they later reported me to SAG, the Screen Actors Guild for my unprofessional behaviour on set. I told SAG the truth of what had occurred and they did not take action against me. I felt such rage that the subject matter was about a real woman, so I felt that there had to be a degree of respect shown. They had no respect for women at all. As to why the director or assistant directors didn't say anything, perhaps they did not want to lose their jobs.

I got through the film, but I never wanted to have anything to do with either of them again. They were trash, totally. Menaham Golan and Yoram Globus; I called them Mayhem and Urine.

And to top it all, the producers didn't even want to spring for a wrap party. So, I threw the wrap party for the cast and crew. Even though the two men had to dirty the experience, I ended up in loving the filming.

## ▌ BESWICK / E

In 1980, Michael Taylor and I took a trip to see his astrologer and numerologist. It was the second time we had been to see her. Michael wanted to see where his life was going at that point. For me at the time, work was a little thin and we were both looking for some answers but without any thinking or hope for a wonderful outlet or result.

Astrology is the study of stars and planets in the sky and how they connect with life on earth. Numerology is the study and practice of assigning meaning to numbers and, through simple calculations, to interpret messages about your life and destiny.

126

The lady was called Betty Collins. She was a fabulous personality, a heavy smoker with a raspy voice and a no-nonsense approach with a raucous laugh. She knew what she was talking about and actually was just great company. She had completed my astrological reading and started my numerological reading. Unfortunately, I didn't and still don't have a time for my birth so she had to work it all out herself, which she did. She picked up on many things in my life. She picked up on my having grown up in Jamaica, who I was and am, my character.

And then, as part of the numerological reading, she said, 'You know, you need to add something here. There is a stop to your work and your money. Why not add an 'e' to your name.'

'Yes,' she continued, 'there does seem to be a block on your monetary life and your work, and I think you need to add some numbers to your name. If we put an 'e' on the end of Beswick, this will give you a different number, and it will make a difference to your work and your money.'

I changed my surname across the board to Beswicke. As an actress, my passport, my driving licence, signatures, autographs, the lot. And that was the year I did a lot of work. It started to flow in, in droves.

I visited her three times in all, but there were other practisers to whom I would go. There was never any frequency to my visits; they were all just when I felt the need. In California, there were many such healers and astrologists. My friend and roommate, Alex, she was also a tarot card reader and numerologist. I would have her read my cards. Or, maybe I would see a healer. One such great healer was Rosalyn Bruyere. She had developed a technique called chelation where she commences the process by running her hands from the feet and up through the body, to run through the various systems and organs until she could see what the problem was, after which she would come up with a treatment. Such was her reputation that she was hired for a film called *Resurrection* as a consultant to instruct the actress, Ellen Burstyn, in the art of spiritual healing and the opening of the mind.

When I came back to London, I found it hard not to have access to astrologists and numerologists in the UK. It was around at that time in England, but it was not nearly as available as in California.

## ■ BUFFALO BILL

*Buffalo Bill* was a US sitcom television series that ran for just two seasons, 1983 and 1984. It starred Dabney Coleman as an egotistical TV talk show host whose unredeemable personality constantly and consistently gave trouble to his long-suffering staff, played by Geena Davies and Joanna Cassidy. Dabney Coleman was hilarious. He had also by then been in the films, *9 to 5* with Dolly Parton, *Wargames* and *On Golden Pond*. I played a Brazilian transsexual; I was a man and very much pre-operation into womanhood. Dabney's character, "Buffalo" Bill Bittinger is getting himself into trouble because he takes a liking to me. I have to tell him I am pre-op and of course, his character freaks out. He was so funny; he was very good at this stuff. His reactions to my character had me literally corpsing all the time, which is to say I was all the time trying not to laugh hysterically.

## ■ COVER UP

*Cover Up* was a one season television series of 22 episodes that aired between 1984 and 1985. Starring Jennifer O'Neill as the wife, Dani Reynolds, the plot follows her investigations into her husband's death and finding out that he was in fact an undercover CIA agent. To help her along the way, she hires a former Special Forces soldier, Mac Harper, played by Jon-Erik Hexum.

The series' production was marred by a tragic on-set accident. John-Erik was this gorgeous model actor with whom I was supposed to have worked. But on the seventh episode of the series, he was waiting on set for the set-up to complete, got bored and was fooling around with a gun that, unbeknown to him, had one blank round left in the chamber. Putting the gun to his head in a Russian Roulette fashion, he pulled the trigger and blew a piece of his skull into his brain. He died in hospital.

Antony Hamilton took over the role of assistant investigator, but as another character, Jack Striker. True to type, I played a wicked woman in the episode, *Black Widow*. Receiving top billing of the guest actors, I was dressed in black and again responsible for killing people while sharing the odd love scene with Anthony's character, Jack. I looked gorgeous, horrible and divine. It was a lovely shoot and everyone, O'Neil, Hamilton and I became longer lasting friends with each other.

I went back to the show a few months later for another episode, *Passions*. We were all terribly excited, the three friends getting together again. I played the same character that had just broken out of jail and was after Jack Stryker. Played for laughs, I had one scene where again, I was dressed all in black, but this time stroking a white cat and threatening them saying, 'If you don't do something or other, I will blow everything up.'

Anthony Hamilton was gay and was dating a friend of mine. They were two good friends that I introduced to Death Valley.

## ◼ DAYS OF OUR LIVES

*Days of our Lives* has the distinction of being one of the longest running soap operas in the world, and I absolutely and positively did not want to do it. And having done it, I knew why.

Commencing in 1965 and running to the present day, UK audiences may be peripherally aware of its existence through being parodied in the hit sitcom *Friends*, where 'Joey' played Dr Drake Ramoray.

By this time, I was represented by another agency, I was put up for the role and in 1984, I needed the work. I did not want to do any of the day time soaps; they were hard work, they were taped and not filmed, and you started at 6am. And bearing in mind that it was a daily running soap from Monday to Friday, each half hour episode was filmed in a day. Mine was a character to play with one of the other top characters.

My first day, I arrived at 6am to be met by the floor manager. 'What's your name; get a pad and the pencil.' 'What?' I ask. She repeated everything verbatim and my heart dropped. Oh oh, this is not going to be fun times. 'Right, let's go; write down everything I tell you and show you.' She was mapping out the floor and showing me where I entered and exited. I knew about hitting marks and blocking, but this was like the orders of an SS person. She should have had a stick and beat me with it. 'Did you get all of that? Right, go to make-up; I'll see you at 6.30. Do it now.'

It was all very confrontational. There was not even a greeting, a hello or a welcome. It was a business. I went to make-up, and it was a heavy make-up. Because the series was taped and not filmed, the set required different lighting techniques and the filming required you to be made up for an entire working day. It was like cement on your face. All the other actors were in the make-up room, chatting away, none of the conversation of which inspired me, at all. The make-up gave me a gigantic infection for which to this day I still have the scar. They took no responsibility for it. The culprit was a dirty sponge.

'Right, now go to your dressing room.' It was all underground. The make-up rooms, the dressing rooms, the studios. I did not see daylight between 6am and 7pm. To keep you awake during the 13-hour days, they turned up the air conditioning and gave you blankets while you waited in your cell.

At my call, I came from my dressing room to set to meet the other actors. Thaao Penghlis, an Australian actor; he played during his time on *Days of our Lives* both André DiMera and Tony DiMera. In ways reminiscent of Joey's character in *Days of our Lives*, Dr Drake Ramoray, who dies and receives a brain transplant from a female character, André is initially introduced as Stefano's nephew who has had plastic surgery to look identical to Stephano's dead stepson, Tony. That Thaao played both parts, and that the original characters were reimagined to fit whatever storyline was being cooked up at the time, was identical to the *Friends* portrayal of Joey Tribbiani's character.

In our script, Thaao played a dresser to a major actor. I am his assistant and we are a pair of killers. We started to work. The producers and director were not on the stage floor. They were in a box watching the acting on a TV screen. They shout that, 'The scene isn't working. Again.' 'Right ok, let's do it again.'

Because Thaao had been in the show for years by then, whenever the shouting and ordering about became just too impossible, he could and would fire back at them. They said, 'We can't go over time, so get it together right now!' And he would fire back, 'We are doing the best we can. Back off!' So, my co-actor had power. But it was all so unnecessarily brutal, and it was constant. I was lucky to have Thaao; without him, I might not have lasted.

At the end of each season, or contract renewal time, everybody was on tenterhooks because someone or some people could be given a pink slip; fired. Everyone was tippy toeing around, wondering if they were going to get fired. And that was the atmosphere the producers created and maintained. The environment was toxic.

Some people have survived for years though. Some have lasted for 20 or more years; the longest serving cast member, Maggie Horton, has been serving the soap since she started in 1973 to present day. Thaao Penghlis had been on the show since 1981 and was in and out of the show, as his various characters were killed and brought back to life until 2009.

I was on and off the soap for two months. And that was long enough. I couldn't do it long term, as soap story lines are always miserable. And you have to learn a full episode Every Day. It was Really heavy. That said, I did do two other soaps, but they were entirely different in that they incorporated the use of locations. They were altogether different.

All this being said, I have nothing but the deepest respect for the actors who do the soaps; it is such hard work. I honestly do not know how they do it.

## ■ MILTON KATSELAS

After the *Days of our Lives* stint, I was worn out, tired, broken, and I needed to oil my machine again; to re-energise myself. I needed to do some more acting classes.

Milton Katselas was an American-Greek director and producer of stage and film, and was also an acting coach and instructor who had trained under one of my other instructors, Lee Strasberg. Milton had created the Beverly Hills Playhouse acting school and his students counted amongst many others, Tom Selleck, Ted Danson, George Clooney, Alec Baldwin, Thaao Penghlis and me.

I figured the costs and I took his classes for two to three months. He made me do *Macbeth*. 'What??' I expostulated. 'Just do it,' he said. And I did. The class was of 30-40 people, no one was there to play around; we were all paying money to do the work. I went through the rehearsals, and I performed the part of the play in front of the entire class in a theatre.

Afterwards, he turned to the class and asked, 'Well, what do you think?' And the class would offer their reviews. 'I felt like she did do something or other...' or, 'I felt like she did not do something else...' They were asked to properly critique. And they could critique you on every brutal level. It could be quite intimidating.

Luckily for me, he turned to audience and said, 'That, people, was excellent.' I was nearly in tears. The emotions you go through as an actress is amazing, in your brain, in your heart; you put it all out there, because if you don't, you know no one will give a shit. He made me work and he was fierce and fair and honest. He gave me the review that I needed.

He was the same as the likes of Peggy Feury and Lee Strasberg; those out there who will make you work, and will beat you up if they feel like you are not giving all of yourself, and if they see that you can do better.

131

It was here that I again fell in love, this time with a gorgeous man with whom I spent a year. Demetre Philips, a Greek, I met him in the class. As time went on, I remember thinking, against all type, maybe this is the one I should marry. As well as the acting, Demetre was a very practical man. I would think, 'He can build a house, he can build a car, maybe this is the kind of person who could take care of me.' There was talk of marriage even though I stipulated that babies were still definitely not on the cards. He was a beautiful man with a wonderful mind, and he was loving. But he was a foundling. As a child, he had been dumped on the doorstep of a Greek priest, abandoned. And as such he had to deal with these issues of abandonment. The priest became his father, and they were very attached to each other. However, when I met the father could not connect with him; he seemed even as a priest, really quite hard and soulless.

He wanted to marry me and I said, 'Let me ask you a question, who do you see marrying us?' 'Well, my father would have to marry us.' I had to say no, not just because of my feelings for his father but the idea of a church wedding and an Orthodox one at that. And so, we broke up. Demetre was more of a builder than an actor and, even though he continued acting in the likes of CHiPs and MacGyver, in the end, that was where his career took him. It was a very difficult breakup; I was very sad and he was devastated. He did meet another lady who he married in the Greek church and with whom they later had a son who I met a few years later. Demetre was a very proud father and I was very happy for him.

## ◼ AIDS

AIDS was reported as having started in 1981, my first friend died of this disease in 1985.

I have many groups of friends, and they can be collated into my different tribes, of which one was my dear Gay Tribe. I had always met and had these people as my friends, and not just in California, also in London. But in California these guys were truly my heart, they were always good fun, they were always incredibly supportive and I loved them dearly. It was almost like having a boyfriend and a girlfriend in the same person and if I was being an alpha male, it meant we sort of matched. I had straight female and male friends and in time, they too became good friends with my gay friends. I am not gay, but I never ruled out the possibility that I might have been attracted to women as well.

These guys, my boys, were overtly sexual, wherever, they went; the infamous bath house, bars and gyms. I was their confidante and even though some of their antics were sometimes quite close to the bone, it nonetheless made me laugh. They were sticking it everywhere. I had already had some affairs with my gay men. Michael and I had had these moments where we found each other physically attractive and celebrated it. It had been the same with Ray and Neil. But then, the guys started to get a bit sick. Something was happening but for whatever reason, they weren't taking any notice. Perhaps they thought they were young and they would bounce back. They were young, so perhaps there was no reason to think otherwise. But something was going on here that certainly made me sit up and notice. Some of the guys were a bit like me in that, once a level of excess had been reached, they would abstain for a period of time so I did tell them, 'You're going to have to pull out for a bit. Rest up.' I was looking in from the outside and I certainly used this as a sign to back off. I stopped smoking, I stopped sex, and I fasted. It was me and my balance button that I had instigated since the frightening event I had had in Jamaica. As it all turned out, lucky me, because had I still been playing with my gay tribe and having affairs, life for me could have been very different.

I saw it all happening before it became public. My intuition told me this was not something people would bounce back from. Then it came into the papers.

Empirical information about AIDS was scant in the early years. And in the vacuum of meaningful information and knowledge, it was filled with rumours and conspiracy theories. Although unsolved to this day, we consider the origins of both HIV-1 and HIV-2, human immunodeficiency virus, to have originated in non-human primates in West-central Africa. In the early 20th century, the diseases were transferred to humans. HIV-1 appears to have originated in wild chimpanzees of southern Cameroon. HIV-2 appears to have originated in the Sooty Mangabey monkeys of the West Africa coast from southern Senegal to western Ivory Coast. These HIV diseases then jumped the species barriers to attack the immune system of human beings which, without treatment, can lead to AIDS, acquired immunodeficiency syndrome. Today, while there is no cure for HIV, people can live with HIV so long as they subscribe to a life-long regimen of medicines. If HIV is allowed to progress to AIDS, the cause of death would be any number of different cancers. As to why it affected gay men more than gay women or straight people, the disease spread more quickly through anal sex and to the receptive partner.

None of which we knew in 1981.

Finally, my tribe had started to get really sick. They were showing lesions, they lost weight; not immediately but a little at a time, and then it would escalate. It was so awful to watch these beautiful men turn into skinny people who could not eat or drink. What the hell was this? It did not happen overnight; it took time. Eventually they were admitted to hospital and put on an awful drug called AZT, otherwise azidothymidine. While administered with the best of intentions in the early years, even with the highest doses that could be tolerated by the patients, AZT was still not strong enough to prevent HIV replication and only slowed the progression of the disease. If that were not upsetting enough, the side effects were equally as horrendous. They included vomiting, nausea, acid reflux, headache, reduction in abdominal body fat, trouble sleeping, loss of appetite, discoloration of fingernails and toenails, mood elevation, occasional tingling or transient numbness of the hands or feet, and minor skin discoloration.

The early stages of the disease were rife with false and misleading reports. The media were rubbish with their reports, they were ignorant at best and inflammatory at worst. AIDS was initially called GRID, gay-related immune deficiency, the gay cancer, and the bible belt jumped all over that one. 'Kill them all,' was their contribution to the situation. That drove me mad. Then there was the thing about not touching infected people. Again, I was furious. The 'touch' thing I did not believe because I was hugging my friends all the time; it was initially clearly a sexually transmitted disease until we understood it could also be transferred through the sharing of needles or blood transfusions. I really appreciated Princess Diana who was photographed hugging some victims to help dispel that myth. The government's stance was like it was their fault, and didn't promote the fact it, at that time, had 'something to do with Africa'.

Still, no one from my tribe of friends had as yet died, but I didn't like the look of it. They were all normally healthy people who, like me, practised the balance thing too. Of course, I hoped they would bounce back. But I had an icky feeling. The intuition was telling me something. I couldn't put my finger on what one could do about all this, but I thought that they were going to die. The AZT drug wasn't the magic bullet we had hoped for.

The guys of course kinda had to stop having sex, and once they had been diagnosed with AIDS, they absolutely couldn't have sex. And anyway, they weren't well enough to have sex. The hope was recovery, but the drug really made them ill in the same way that chemotherapy lays you low. In some cases, it was even worse. When the guys had started to take the drug, I think they started to see the end; that they wouldn't come out of this. It was one thing to get older, the aging process. It was entirely another thing to deal with a disease that is eating you from the inside out, to turn you into a wraith.

As my boys deteriorated, some wanted to let go and tried to commit suicide. Those that could still eat, sleep and talk did not let go. It was a really tough for the families. It numbed me to death. The first death I experienced was when I was in my 20s, and was the 16-year-old son of an ex of John's. He came to visit John and we had become friends. Unfortunately, he was a heroin addict and sadly overdosed. In my 30s, Michael Taylor's sister, Gayle, overdosed at the age of 23 on the infamous coke-heroin cocktail.

And then we were in the 1980s and I was having to come to terms with losing so many of my dearest friends. My heart was broken so often, I wondered if it would ever heal, and if there were any tears left.

When Michael Taylor died, we had a memorial, and we decided none of us would wear black. We all wore prints and colours, to celebrate life and his life. We quickly learned to celebrate the loss, even if a part of your heart was bleeding.

We watched the lesions and weight loss take over Neil Lavelle. He went home to his family of 12 and once he passed, we scattered his ashes in Death Valley. Again, we were all in colours and shorts and we related funny stories to each other about him.

Learning, accepting, celebrating and loving.

I certainly became careful, and I made sure the guys understood they had to wear their little balloons whether they liked that or not. But in the end, and quite coincidentally, I had a partner. It was not an affair, and it meant that there were only two people in our little equation.

My Gay Tribe who died through AIDS.
RIP

Buddy Micucci – Roy's Bartender
Michael Taylor – Model / Actor
Neil Dillard – boyfriend to Michael Taylor
Neil Lavelle – Michael's friend, I called him my husband
Bobby Consolmagnio – boyfriend to Neil Lavelle
Bill Hudnut – Comedian, singer, comedy class instructor
Tim Hawkins – A friend who was peripheral to the industry
Ray Underwood – was for a period Michael's lover
Billy Porter – Yoga teacher
Anthony Hamilton – Actor, Cover Up

## ◼ THE IMPOSSIBLE LOVE FOR ACTING

In 1984, work was again a little thin on the ground, but the realities of rent, car and food were ever present.

I didn't want to go back to waitressing. I had done it once. One of my gay boys, Greg Padgett, who lived near the Ranch and was a constant visitor, was a wonderful artist who painted on fabrics. It gave me the idea to create sarongs.

Against my car, I borrowed $2600 and I began my little business. I was very excited. I found the perfect fabrics, hired a seamstress and Greg and I created the designs together. They were really beautiful but not cheap. I approached swimwear boutiques in Malibu and LA. I even did photographic sessions to demonstrate the different ways to wear them but the truth is that it was a business that I had never done before and my business brain was not great. I lasted three to four months. While I knew business people who could perhaps have helped me master a business, they were not from this business. It wasn't going to happen. I probably sold 50, but all to my friends.

The money had gone.

My next idea was The Sweetheart Company. My friends needed help with kids, to pick stuff up, to perform errands. I would be a freelance assistant, but just with and for my friends. I would file stuff, post things, do the laundry, get the shopping, all the things that families needed help with. I had been doing this as a friend but now I started to charge. The car needed gas, and the rent needed to be paid. I explored helping people who needed to move home. The first time I did it, I rented and drove a truck to move a girlfriend of mine, Diantha Lebenzon, whose walls were decorated with serious works of art.

I asked her if she had made any arrangements to move and she blithely said, 'Oh, I have picked up some Safeway boxes to start packing.' I said, 'Darling, don't be ridiculous. I will organise your move for you, obviously for a fee. I will hire a truck and pack it all.' She happily agreed. It was a bit scary. I rented and drove the truck, purchased all the packing materials, and hired two of my out-of-work best friends. I proceeded to begin my first move.

I learned a lot from my foray into this new venture. I ended up organising a professional moving company who did the actual move and supplied all the necessary materials. My job was to pack and unpack the entire contents of the house. I actually enjoyed doing this as it allowed me to be creative. Through my friends and word of mouth, I was kept busy. My new business card was simply, Personal Mover. And it really was just that. It was hard work, and also intimate, literally living with my clients for periods of weeks, sometimes months. They appreciated my organisational skills and my boundless energy. This was a new discovery of myself. I did look into making it into a proper business. But the trucks and the insurance cost too much. I managed to pay the money back to the bank manager on my car loan.

I have been asked questions such as; was there ever a consideration towards some sort of financial security? Did you ever want to buy a house, or feel the need to invest in such? Were you ever able to save, invest, or create a pension? And if so, did you ever feel perhaps you needed to find another career to support that? All of which were perfectly reasonable questions, for someone else.

There had been a moment whereby a friend was desperate for some help in an office. I had been in an office in London. By now this was not something entirely alien to me. My friend needed at short notice, a receptionist. 'Help me,' he had said, with eyes and tones that could not be refused. After one week in that office, I had wanted to kill myself. 'I can never do this ever again,' I had admitted to myself. 'It just is not my scene, to answer phones and look at a wall for an eight-hour day. I would rather be poor and counting pennies, than going into an office,' I assured myself.

And here's the thing that maybe no one else can possibly imagine. I was passionately in love with acting; I loved loved loved it. There was always the excitement of getting the part. I'VE GOT IT. For reasons unknown, I had wanted this, absolutely This, from when I was a little girl, the excitement experienced from being in front of a camera, it kept you going, the promise of that magical moment when all of the acting stars aligned that opened the gates for the nuances to flow between the actors, or even within yourself. It might also be as experienced when a musical band jams, or might be as experienced when a football team melds towards a common flow, or as a driver feels as man and car kiss the apex at everyone's and everything's limit; just maybe as an actor you would experience this inexplicable feeling just once in a film, or just once in a TV episode. One little moment when everything is right, and you feel it is right, and everyone around you on the set or on the location feels it is right; it is something that not only keeps you going, it is something that makes you want to do better and to have that feeling again. And then you start to look for those moments. When it's not right, My God, why could

I have not done it differently, or better? I am not alone in thinking this.

Being the lead or star on your own TV show has its own responsibilities. The cast, crew and audience expect that person to 'carry' the show. But being the guest star has its own huge responsibilities to come up with the goods, hit the marks, know the lines, and be on time; all at the same time as when a tight knit cast and crew are looking at you and thinking, Oh God, who is this woman? But then, you concentrate on the joy of creating characters on screen. It is part of the excitement of it all. And when you get it right, you can feel it through the whole crew, and that initial question turns into, Oh wow.

Being an actress is interesting. You have you, and only you. You have no hammer, no wrench, no tools. You are the tool. And it means everything.

Returning to the above questions, the security I did not bother with. You understood that unless you could get a series that would provide other means, you would be a working actor. With a series, all was good. Mine was piece work. I might be paid $3000 for a week's work, and then nothing for a month. That could then lead to scrabbling around for rent and bills, and that is when other side hustles helped. But you stayed with acting. I stayed with acting.

I always looked to see what else I could do, but it would always be as well as acting, and not in place of. Times were, and could be really hard. I would write in my diary, Black Day, or Grey Day, but it is a day. It does hit you. Sometimes you even would go to the SAG to ask for a loan. Sometimes, you had to sign on for unemployment, and you would see your friends on the same line. And then suddenly a show could pay you $10,000 and you would be ok for several months. On a yearly basis however, one could see it as being hand to mouth.

LA catered to a lot of English actors, actors with bigger names. For example, Judy Geeson. 'Hello darlings,' we would greet each other. 'How are you, may the best lady win,' was the truth of it. I had Bond and Hammer but, there was always a bigger name. And that was the reality. You have got to have some balls to be in this business. It is quite brutal, but then the passion for acting would keep you going. It is precisely this that kept me going.

Another question was asked of me. Bearing in mind I had by then travelled from Jamaica to London, to Jamaica and back to London. Then in search of acting to LA and then Rome and back here to LA, could I have travelled again? There were no other places to look for work. The Americans had left London; in Rome I would have had to have started all over again. At this juncture, there could never any possibility, or intention, to look for fresh shores. So, LA it had to be. I had a name for episodic TV, I was called several times by name but even then, you might not get the part. I would come in, chat, but then others might demand someone else gets the part. The final decision was never just the director or producer; the studio and the network, those two are enormously powerful. If they don't want you, you won't get it. You are up against it at every level. But here's the thing. The passion for acting prevents what might be for others to be the obvious route out.

And just when life seems to be at its hardest, I was introduced to residuals. Residuals are payments that an actor, director or writer can earn when their work is reused beyond the one time for which it was initially only going to be aired. Reruns, second lives on cable or satellite, or if the program was sold to another network all contributed to the residuals, so the more shows you did, the more sources of perpetual income you would have. When you would least expect it, $2000 would come in.

Maybe I could have not paid to go so often to Death Valley, or eat the best food, but this was not me. Had I counted pennies, maybe something would be different, but maybe that would have been for a different person. Enjoyment of life trumped counting. And, a part of you has got to have that attitude to be the person to do the job. No regrets.

### ■ THE SHELL GAME

*The Shell Game* was an American comedy-drama television series that ran from January to February, 1987. Consisting of just six episodes, the premise followed the exploits of former husband and wife former con artists played by James Reid and Margot Kidder as they try to expose crooks for what they are. Against his will, Read's Riley is drawn into conning the bad guys by Kidder's Dinah for the good of society; something that Dinah hopes will reunite them. I appear in the fourth episode, *Upstairs Gardner*, where I play a rich woman, Mrs. Susan Bonne. Married to my husband, I had found he was not to be trusted and, in the meantime, I am having an affair with our gardener, Pedroza, as played by Benicio del Toro. I discover that my husband has been removing my art from the walls of our house and replacing them with forgeries; the originals to have been sold for his financial benefit. I confront him with this fact, threaten to expose him, and he murders me. But it is the gardener who is arrested for the crime.

However, the scene starts with me in bed with Del Toro. We are half naked and interrupted by my husband's arrival, 'Oh my husband's home.' A brash young man, this was Del Toro's first screen appearance. While we were in bed, he said, 'Why don't you ask me out? Take me to dinner.' I was twice his age and I said, 'No.' He took it well; he knew he was trying it on. It was probably his thing.

## ■ CYCLONE

A B-movie that took just 18 days to film, inventor Rick has developed a $5m motorcycle that is equipped with rocket launchers and laser guns, and which needs only oxygen as fuel. It is called the Cyclone. Government funded, criminal arms dealers become aware of the bike's charms and wish it for their own less socially-minded purposes. Rick is murdered and it is down to his partner, Teri, to ensure, all by her lonesome, that the bike does not fall into the wrong hands. Jeffrey Coombs and Heather Thomas play the leads. I play this time, not a baddie but an FBI agent.

It was directed by Fred Olen Rey, a top low-budget film producer, director and screenwriter of over 200 such films. He was also very good at getting top actors to play minor roles in his films and this one featured Martin Landau and an uncredited Russ Tamblyn. It was all shot on location on the streets of LA and everyone gave it their all. I might have auditioned for the part but Fred wanted the people he wanted and I think he had already decided.

## ■ FROM A WHISPER TO A SCREAM

Also called *The Offspring, From a Whisper to a Scream* was an anthology film of four different and unconnected horror stories. After a prologue that showed a lady called Kathryn White being killed by lethal injection for murder, these four stories are relayed to a local journalist, Beth Chandler, by an old historian, and Kathryn's uncle, Julian White, as played by Vincent Price. Once the four stories have been related, Beth reveals to Julian that she had been contact with Kathryn while she was in jail awaiting her demise, and had been impressed upon the fact that Julian might have poisoned Kathryn's mind with murder that led to her own killing. Beth then kills Julian.

I played the niece to Vincent Price's character. I had not met Vincent before, even when we had both filmed for Hammer. When I met him, he was sitting in a make-up chair with a knife through his throat. That was how I met him and he was just lovely, such a gentleman and an epicurean. 'You realise we have been both in Hammer,' I opened. 'And I have your cookbook'. I still have it; a huge leather-bound two-inch tome of a book, and I have used it several times.

My character had to die. I had no idea how I was going to play this. Dying is not easy as an actor. You have to try to leave your body. It is not just about closing your eyes and stopping breathing. Also, I had to ask myself, how do I react to having a lethal injection? I thought, well, it is a drug; I have had a few of those. I will bring back a memory of one of those times and use that. I did and it worked quite well. I also brought a bit of madness, I started to shake, while I was dying, I considered a memory I had of me dancing with someone. As I am going out of it, I listened to the music in my head, that was all lovely, the music and my death. It was my version of dying by lethal injection.

The film was directed by Jeff Burr, another lovely young man. He was again one of the well-known directors for low-budget films. His team were terrific; he later went on to film *The Texas Chainsaw Massacre III* and the *Puppet Master* films. He was very young at the time of filming our movie, only 24 and very creative. I ran into him a few times at the various film conventions. He died only aged 60, in Ohio.

## ◼ SLEDGE HAMMER!

This two-season television series was just bonkers. A parody of Inspector Callahan of the Dirty Harry films, the series follows the adventures of a deranged and dumb police detective who always looks for the most exaggeratedly violent solution to any problem. Mayhem and a twisted sense of humour was the series' forte.

I played Lana, a mob boss, pool shark and killer in the 1987 first season episode, *The Color* [sic] *of Hammer*. My character blackmails and then murders a hard-line judge when he fails to pay her the money she is owed after hustling him over a game of pool. Sledge Hammer and his partner Dori Doreau investigate which leads them to the pool establishment and Lana. Lana then challenges Sledge Hammer to a game and after winning the first one, she then loses $50,000. Pulling a stiletto from her cue stick to kill Sledge it is written that the best place to hold this fight is actually on the pool table. Sledge defeats Lana by rolling a cue ball towards Lana which she then steps on and falls backwards. As I said, nuts.

She is led away by the police along with her henchmen.

I had to have pool lessons for this role. It was already a game that I quite liked having been to nightclubs that had a pool room whereby, after the drinking and dancing, pool offered some quiet respite. However, for the playing of all the major shots I had to have a proper pool champion take over. But she was left-handed. So not only did I have to appear professional with a cue, but to match her shots, I had to do it left-handed too. I was very excited. One shot required me do a shot blind. I did it and the ball went into the damn hole. I had to perform shots from behind my back. And I had to do it all in 1950s outfits.

I do not know why I got such a profusion of killer type roles. Maybe it was the way I looked. At the time, I didn't know what a feminist was but I probably was one. Women were looked down upon, the kitchen being the best place for them and I had an anger about all that stuff. Maybe it was always an underlying thing in my life which materialised in my persona. I was happy with the roles though and I preferred playing the baddy; they were always the better roles.

Although in *Thunderball* I was a victim. Very upsetting…

## ◼ MIAMI BLUES

*Miami Blues* is a little 1990 black comedy drama starring Alec Baldwin as a recently released sociopath and thief, Fred Ward and Jennifer Jason Leigh. Produced by friends, Jonathan Demme and Gary Goetzman, it was they who gave me a part in their film. We have lost Jonathan, but Gary is still to this day one of the Hollywood good guys who, together with Tom Hanks, another Hollywood good guy, have their own production company.

I played a restaurant waitress who had to give Alec Baldwin's character a hard time. Hard looks, and everything I had to say was a line loaded with sarcasm and faintly disguised venom. I didn't figure on playing a stroppy as a waitress, but they pushed me to do it. A small but lovely part, it was all shot on location in Miami. And this was where I got to swim with dolphins.

Gary's wife, Leslie, and I went to Grassy Key and the Dolphin Research Centre; a centre whose mission it is to promote peaceful coexistence, cooperation and communication between marine mammals, humans, and our environment. It was a magical moment. We were instructed to get into the water, a pool, with three dolphins. Staying still, the dolphins would then come to you and to suss you out. And when they were ready, you were instructed to hang on to their fins for a ride in the enclosed area. There were three dolphins and three people in the pool at same time. For some reason, all three dolphins concentrated themselves around me and ignored the two other people. No one else was being offered a ride. It was a bizarre but wonderful experience. They would nose me along; they would turn me around and get me into a position for the ride they wanted to next offer. This really was a most glorious and magical moment. I think I was in the water with them for a half an hour, maybe not quite an hour. The feel of the dolphins is so gorgeous; their skin is like silk and satin. I rubbed them, and they would kiss you. It was such a sweetness. One of the dolphins was pregnant.

One of the carers said, 'It is time for you to leave'. I didn't want to; I couldn't leave them alone. 'You must leave now.' Finally, I started making my way to the ladders to get out. I was in my bikini, and the pregnant dolphin came up behind me and pushed me up and out of the water. Words failed me.

Dolphin Magic

## COMMERCIALS

As well as working in film and television, acting in commercials was also very much a part of the survival technique required to get you through the year, with the added bonus that the work contributed to the acting process. Acting in a commercial is still a performance, it sits within the bounds of acting, they are quickies that are set up and filmed very efficiently, and they pay very well. It was almost essential to have commercials as part of your earnings portfolio. And they were also productions whereby one received residuals, nice ones too.

There would on occasion be commercials that offered a buyout; a flat fee that would not subscribe to the residual formula. Instead of $1000, the buyout fee would be $1500. And it would be a take it or leave it approach. There was never a choice. I preferred the commercials that offered residuals for those surprise cheques that would more often than not come just at the right time. There was no rule of thumb as to how it all worked, but the bigger jobs would more likely be residual based. The smaller jobs tended not to play country-wide.

I had by now two agents, a Commercial agent and a Regular film and TV agent. You had to. All the opportunities could come in really fast, but you wouldn't necessarily pick everything up as there were thousands of us. Maybe I did three or four commercials a year. I kept my Commercial agent for a long time; Sonia Brandon Lewis of Commercials Unlimited. She was superb.

Lazer Tag had its birth in 1979. South Bend Electronics released the toy, Star Trek Electronic Phasers, which then morphed into a recreational sport whereby teams of people 'shoot' each other in a controlled environment with infrared emitting light guns. Evolving into indoor and outdoor events that further evolved into local, regional, national and international tournaments, Lazer Tag was on the up and up. They advertised prolifically. And the productions were huge.

I was hired, but before anything happened, I had to sign an NDA. The set up was that of a huge dystopian Colosseum filled with many competitors all dressed in leather outfits. It was a very kinetic presentation, where everyone was always moving and on the go. The competitors were first called to arms in the arena and I played the master of ceremonies that created the energy of the atmosphere and announced, 'Let the games begin.'

It was very much like a Ridley Scott production, hard lighting, cold colours and very exciting. All the other actors were really excited by it. It was all filmed in five days.

The following year, I did another commercial for Lazer Tag whereby the game was again played in a Colosseum, but this time shaped as a skateboarders' bowl. The competitors were skateboarders where they would ride and shoot as they went. The kineticism had just been upped tenfold with skaters flying over the top

Dressed in leather for Lazer Tag

The Dominatrix surrounded by her musclemen prootectors for West

of each other, and me shouting orders at everyone. Again, it was really beautiful.

West was a German tobacco and cigarette manufacturer that was created in 1981. Their campaign slogans were 'Let's go West', and, later in 1986, 'Test the West'; snappy, catchy, and relatively innocent.

The brand came to LA to do some creative thinking for an advertising campaign that would be shown in Germany.

I am not too sure what the thinking was behind the photographic campaign, certainly bearing in mind the innocence of the slogans above, and certainly bearing in mind the message that their campaign would be sending, and certainly bearing in mind how today cigarettes are not even advertised. But, their theme had me dressed as a dominatrix and whipping to within an inch of his life a smoker. The photographer was a German fashion photographer and film director called Peter Lindbergh. He would work with Linda Evangelista, Naomi Campbell, Cindy Crawford, Christy Turlington, and would later photograph the Pirelli Calendar three times.

For this shoot, he had me dressed in a leathered outfitted, on the streets of LA, and on a raised platform whipping this hapless chap. Even though this was still photography, I had to create a sense of movement and far below me, on the ground, people were watching what was going on, and praying for me. Well, one lot were clapping me, but others were praying for me.

The photography campaign evidently did the trick because I was asked back not only for a filmed video commercial, but later a personal appearance. The commercial replicated in video what we had done with the photography and then I was asked to fly to Cologne in Germany for an appearance at a trade show to perpetuate the dominatrix character.

The trade show seemed to be a lifestyle affair where promoters of cigarettes would sit alongside promoters of clothes. It was a huge venue, it had nice lighting, and each company had their own production space. This did not involve any professional photography or videography, but did again involve me, as my character, dressed as a West-sash wearing dominatrix and wandering around the exhibition hall to attract attention. And attract I did.

I had with me at all times, four weightlifter bodyguards who were bare chested and wore tight pants. One of the bodyguards took a shine to me. I was wearing high-heeled thigh-high boots and my feet were killing me, so he just lifted me to wherever I had to go. If needed to go to loo, they had to take me there. Otherwise, dressed as I was, people would have come after me and undoubtedly there would be a problem. Indeed, even with the imposing presence of the four weightlifters I had people approach me who wanted to be whipped. 'Could you please whip me?' And I did; I was quite nice to them; I didn't hurt them. Me dressed like this really brought out people's weird fantasies. My guys would say, 'Well, just pretend; just give them a little whipping.' There was a moment when I was going to the ladies' room, the bodyguards were around me, huge muscles, tights; they were massive and imposing. As we were walking along, somebody managed to slip through the cordon to get to me. Well, my bodyguards and I, we turned on him. I was about to whip him, he grabbed the whip, and I really got into it. He was ready to have the shit whipped out of him, but my lovely men, they picked me up and spirited me away.

This lasted three days. Three days of standing around and being a dominatrix, with a whip, boots and high heels. Every couple of hours, I would be given a break. I realise that perhaps there could have been a requirement for some continuity between the first photographic advert, the second video advert and this personal appearance. But nonetheless, I was amazed that they called me, and shipped me in to do this. And all the people I had met before, they were lovely people, they took me out to dinner afterwards. It blew my mind as I was by then in my late 40s, all decked out as this character.

The commercials continued to pay good money. Honda hired me on three separate occasions in one year for two car adverts and one motorcycle advert. Four of us played aliens who were visiting planet earth and didn't know what fun was. All four of us were of course bald headed, the three men and me. During make-up, we were all terribly calm but the absurdity of the situation would lead to on-set laughter and the eternal deterioration of our abilities to maintain a professional approach. We got it in the end.

## ▮ EVIL SPIRITS

*Evil Spirits* is a 1991 film directed by Gary Graver and starring Karen Black as Ella Purdey, a strange woman who runs a boarding house whose misfit tenants wouldn't be missed if they happened to die. And die they do. Ella continues to cash in their government benefit cheques even after they have disappeared. I played a character called Vanya who had to give a séance at a table surrounded by the other house guests. Having gone into a meditation for the scene, I actually felt as if I was being invaded by evil spirits; the very enacting of the scene was bringing it all into me. It was a low budget affair and I think it only took 10 days to film, which for such was quite a long shoot.

Karen Black played her character like all the characters she played, always offbeat and eccentric. While most people apply stage make-up to lessen the shine in the lights, it appeared Karen applied Vaseline to her face. For what reason no one ever knew but it led to 'behind the hand' chat. We all left her to do her own thing. She was odd, but she really was excellent.

Around the same time, Terence Young came into town. By now he was married to the French actress, Sabine Sun, a big blond woman with a wonderful and bold sense about her. They had met each other on one of his films. We spent several days together doing double cinema evenings and dinners. He really was The most elegant gentleman I had ever met. Everything about him was perfect; how he was dressed and how he held himself. He had a good stature; a man who was very much happy in his own skin. I adored him. This might have been the last time I ever saw him.

## ◼ TRANCERS II: THE RETURN OF JACK DETH
A 1991 sequel to the 1984 *Trancers*, the film is notable for one of Helen Hunt's very earliest performances and for the actor comedian, Tim Thomerson, who played the eponymous Deth.

Low budget and straight to video, we filmed on location in LA. I played one of three baddies, Nurse Trotter. Thomerson was by then 45 years of age but was already looking well weathered. His character shared scenes with a back-from-the-dead wife played by Megan Ward who was 22, and the new wife played by Helen Hunt who was 28. It was that kind of movie. The following year, Helen Hunt would get her breakthrough role in the sitcom, *Mad About You*.

Tim Thomerson was also a stand-up comic whose wit was bone dry. There was a scene where a group of us were walking towards a camera that was backing up. We are striding, we are looking purposeful and we are committing to the B moment. Tim was positioned just behind the camera to feed us his words but also for our eye line; a position that all of us in the walking group could focus on. But he would say a word, and it would be said in a way that would have us in hysterics.

149

We would have to do it again and again. We none of us could keep a straight face. The director was so pissed off.

## ▮ WIDE SARGASSO SEA

Written by Jean Rhys, the 1966 novel of the same name is one of my absolute and of all-time favourite novels. Rhys was British but had been born in the Caribbean island of Dominica. I have read it many times. The story follows a Creole heiress, Antoinette Cosway, as she considers her unhappy marriage to Mr Rochester, in an environment of post-colonial relationship powers between men and women, slavery and race. The book plays out in Jamaica.

Jean writes her books in such a way that you feel yourself to be there, to be able to touch the plants, to smell the flowers, to be right in the middle of the environment of which she writes. I like going somewhere in my books and she does it brilliantly. I have read all of her books, and they are all different. I am, it is fair to say, a big reader. My shelves are creaking with books, even though I try clear out on occasion and take them to the charity shop.

Post-colonialism, race, Jamaica, plantations were all close to my heart and I was always interested in doing my best to be a part of a screen adaptation of this book. I had met Michael Apted in the 1960s many years previous to this film. Michael Apted was lined up to direct the film and conversations had been held which looked as though they would lead to my playing Antoinette Cosway and Michael York to play Mr Rochester. But as so often in the ways of film making, this adaptation never came to be.

Jan Sharp was a friend of mine and was married to director Phillip Noyce. I met Jan again in 1991 and she was now trying to raise the finances to make the film. My heart began pounding because I wanted to be in the film. Obviously now I was too old to play the lead role but Jan said, 'I want you to play Antoinette Cosway's Aunt Cora.' I was so excited, and then I discovered that Michael York was also cast in the older role of Paul Mason.

Karina Lombard of The Firm would star as Antoinette Cosway, and Nathaniel Parker would play Edward Rochester. This was almost going to be like my swan song, to be doing my favourite book.

I met the Australian director John Duigan on April 21st and from then to the middle of June, I had many meetings with the costume designer, Norma

Moriceau, of Mad Max fame, and the make-up artist who was actor Sam Neil's wife, Noriko Watanabe. As the film covers a number of years, I had to age, which meant differing costumes and I also had to be fitted for a wig. We arrived in Jamaica on June 29th in the north western Cornish parish of Trelawny, an area best known for its sugar estates and sugar cane mills.

We undertook four days of rehearsals, and we started shooting July 11th. I finished my work in a month.

*Wide Sargasso Sea* could, and should, have been a brilliant film, but I think John Duigan was overwhelmed by the power of us, the women. Also including Rachel Ward, there were some powerhouse women in the film. We were a team, but that sense did not necessarily come out in the film. The film was steamy, sensual and erotic. John found himself surrounded by strong women and this might not have been his usual experience or his comfort zone. At one point, having already sensed this, I went up to him and said, 'John, you have a fantastic cast, and you need to bring it out of all of us.' I don't think he allowed our power to hit the screen. At times, I felt like I was being word read, which is to say I would be given the exact rendition of the words, and then to just reiterate them as opposed to acting. It came across as an undermining of our acting abilities, in my opinion. In the end the film did not receive the reviews that it should have gained. It was a shame as something was certainly missing. But in other films, John definitely had the goods.

John Duigan was later to have said that he did not enjoy making the film. He said, 'It was probably the only really unsatisfying interaction that I've had with a production company and I found that I had major disagreements with them and with the producers. It was unfortunate. Jan Sharp, the producer of the film, had the tenacity to get the film made, but she and I had differences of opinion. She was very well informed on the book, and I'm sure her opinions were arguable, as I like to think mine were, but when you have a situation like that, I think the overall project can suffer. I think the film did suffer from that division.'

During the filming, every Sunday, us girls; Norma Moriceau, Karina Lombard, Claudia Robinson, Kimberley Addams, the assistant costume designer, and I would go rafting on the Martha Brae River and have a picnic. It became our thing. After filming, I spent some time in Negril by myself, just two days. I had a little hut on the beach right next to the water. I am not a big swimmer, but the waters were lovely and warm. All of a sudden, a rather lovely young man with dreadlocks sidled up to me in the water and asked if he could swim with me. Now these young men are known as Rent-a-Rastas. Basically, gigolos who were looking to have a nice lady take them to America or England. So, I turned on him with my proper Jamaican accent, and said, 'Listen 'ere bouy, you know who you talkin' to?' With a shocked and sheepish look on his face, he turned away and did a typical Jamaican action called 'kiss 'im teet', a sucking teeth action that has many meanings but, in this case, 'Okay lady, a goin''. He swished off in the water.

The brilliant costume designer, Norma Moriceau, and I on our day off from filming *Wide Sargasso* in Jamaica

On September 26th, I had a big 50th birthday bash in LA and Steve Counsel, my live in partner, gave me a ring and exclaimed 'I would like to engage you.' A perfect fun present for my 50th. Neither of us was exactly the marrying kind except a few years later, after we ended, he did get married.

We stayed together for six and half years even though my friends didn't really approve of him. I had met him at a party in 1990 held by English film music composer, Peter Robinson. I was looking at Peter's wispy girlfriend and commented to myself, 'She is a Twiggy, and now I am a Jane Russell.' And this voice behind me said, 'I love Jane Russell.' He was younger than me by 16 years, and had the same mad hair as Rod Stewart. It was a fiery relationship, and even more so when we finally moved in together.

## ■ RODNEY KING

Rodney King was a black man who had been battling with alcohol and drug addiction through the 1980s and 1990s. By 1991, he had been pulled over many a time for a variety of driving offences exacerbated by his addictions. It was also a period of time when there were increasing racial tensions between the African American and Korean American communities, and increasing complaints from minority communities of harassment and use of excessive force by the Los Angeles Police Department.

On 3rd March 1991, Rodney King and two passengers were driving through the San Fernando Valley when the California Highway Patrol signalled to them to pull over. Rodney King had just been released from prison for robbery, assault and battery, and he knew being caught by the authorities would violate his parole. A high-speed chase ensued that took them through the Lake View Terrace neighbourhood. Two CHP officers arrested King and the two other occupants.

Five LAPD officers took over the arrest; three Caucasians and two Hispanics. Still in Lake View Terrace, the five officers tasered King, struck him, kicked him, tackled him to the ground and then handcuffed his wrists and hogtied his legs. All of which was filmed by a local resident from the window of his apartment in Hansen Dam. The 12 minutes of footage showed that every time King tried to get up, he was struck again. He was only cuffed when he remained still.

By April 1992, there followed a court case brought by the Los Angeles County District Attorney against four of the five officers. There were no African American jury members and there was only one Latin American jury member. On 29th April after seven days of jury deliberation, all four officers were acquitted of assault and three of the four officers were acquitted of using excessive force. A verdict could not be achieved for the fourth officer in this last.

As soon as the verdicts were announced on the 29th April, the Rodney King riots began. Also known as the 1992 Los Angeles riots, there began five days of rioting, looting, arson and assault that resulted in 63 deaths, 2383 injuries and property damage of over $1 billion.

And I was right in the middle of all of it.

I was in my apartment in Hancock Park with Alexandra Summer and my partner, Steve Counsel, and watched LA erupt. The California National Guard and the

United States Military were brought in to help resolve the situation and curfews were put in place between dusk and dawn. It was bedlam. We watched the fires commencing and escalating from our back door. It was awful and bloody terrifying. We were right in thick of it. Frankly, if they hadn't have brought in the National Guard, there would have been a civil war. None of us had ever experienced this before, the power and destruction of racial tensions.

We were holed up for the duration. Perhaps we left the apartment only for provisions. We were never physically threatened even while being right in the thick of it, but, perhaps redundantly, we maintained a hose in case the fires started to come too close to us; not that in retrospect, a hose could have done much good at all.

## ■ SISTER AND FILM FESTIVAL

I was still receiving reports on the welfare of my sister. In August 1992, I went to London to see her. The process was still the same, as was any meaningful and long-term progress. She was still in and out of care on a regular basis. When she was in care, she would recover sufficiently to be released and while she was out for period, she was great; she was funny, she was adored, she told funny stories. And then of course, the manic depression would hit her again, and again she would have to go back into care for help. It had been her desire to get married and have lots of children. Instead, she became second mama to her friends' children. Elsa and Roderick Peters, their daughter was named Fuchsia Laurellie, and my sister adored her. Actress, Gabriella Lucidi (Married name, Schneck), whose son, Matthew, was also much adored. Unfortunately, Gabriella died in 2023. Elsa, who was a dear friend from Jamaica, worked very closely with Chris Blackwell as a right-hand woman.

It was good to see my sister again. I stayed for the entire month of August. As well as seeing my sister, I also caught up with my London friends who had not come to LA. I saw the actor singer John Leyton and his wife Dini; John had been in The Great Escape and Von Ryan's Express. I saw my very good friend, Jeremy Clyde and his mother, Eliza. And I made sure to see Francine Winham, the debutante who had lived with us in Connaught Square and had become in her own right a film director producer.

In October, I was invited to attend the Sitges Film Festival in the Catalonia area of Spain. I went with my friend Evelyn Purcell who at the time was married to Jonathan Demme. They were, both personally and professionally, quite a team.

She also produced some of his early films and was second unit director as well. She went on to be a film director in her own right. The Sitges Film Festival turned out to be a big deal as the film festival had its origins in horror and fantasy and had been going since 1971. Of course, I had been invited because of my Hammer House of Horror films. I was flown in and provided accommodation and expenses. Every day for nine days, I was brought on stage for a series of Q&As and to promote Hammer Horror. I was also a judge for one of the films in competition.

It was also where I met Quentin Tarantino, who was showing *Reservoir Dogs* in competition and for which he won Best Director. Tim Roth was also in attendance. It was Quentin's first film and he was hugely excited and massively effusive. He was like a kid in a candy store, like he was 13 years old. It turned out he was a fan of mine, and although I went up a couple of times for his movies, of which one was *Jackie Brown*, it never quite worked out.

## ROBBED

In 1993 I was in LA and coming home from a dinner. I was in a good mood, I hadn't been drinking, I was relaxed and I was walking towards my apartment at 131 Sycamore in Hancock Park. I was walking towards my front door and I saw a cat. 'Hello pussy,' I greeted him. I didn't see anyone.

In LA, and perhaps anywhere in the world, you always had to be aware of everything around you. Walk with a sense of purpose, do not look lost, do not invite opportunity and don't carry valuables in the open. But on this occasion, I was not concerned as I was right next to my door and supposed security. I had not experienced any sixth sense feeling. I was about to put the keys in my front door when two hooded kids leapt in front of me. 'Give me your bag.' I saw the gun.

And that should have been the point where I just gave them my bag. 'But there's nothing in it,' I said. One of the kids ripped the bag off me in such a way that I was left with just the bag strap on my shoulder.

They were young, they wore hoods, it was dark. My flatmate, Alexandra Summer and my partner, Steve Counsel, were horrified when I told them what had just happened. We called the police. They immediately arrived and took my statement, but there was precious little they could do. I called the bank to stop all my cards, which was such a pain. At least I still had my car and house keys although the reality of what could have happened was very sobering.

But then, I became angry, I was also really sad for these two young kids. Maybe they were 14. I had so many contrasting emotions; no fear now, just anger. Why did they put themselves in that situation, I asked myself. I too could have had a gun. They were weird emotions to have. I didn't understand why I felt sad; in fact, I also found it slightly funny in that I had been left only with the bag strap on my shoulder. They could have shot me though as I saw they were really nervous. Of course I should have said, 'Here, take the bag.'

Bizarrely though, or perhaps contrastingly to the event I had just experienced, no one then thought of getting a gun in the classic way of slamming shut the barn door after the criminals had bolted. I did not know anyone who carried a gun, and it certainly did not make me feel like carrying a gun. As a Green Card holder, I was not allowed to have a pistol. When John Richardson and I were living together, he thought I should have had some sort protection when he went off for a film. We bought a shotgun and we put it under the bed. I had never thought about getting a shotgun. Having bought it, I went to the ranges to practice with it and to know how it felt. We went a few times, and actually I was reasonably good at it.

In ways contrary to the above experience, the first week he was away, someone actually did try to break into the house. I retrieved the gun from under the bed, stuck it to the door and yelled, 'I have a gun!' They heard me, and they ran off. I was shaking, freaking out. I couldn't believe it. It had always been my nightmare for someone to break in and to assault or perhaps rape me. I put the gun back under the bed, and that was the last time it ever came out. I have no idea where it went after we left LA. It didn't come to England or Rome with us.

## CONVENTIONS

Film fairs and Conventions had been around since the 1970s. These are events where organisers can bring people from the world of film to meet people who are interested in the world of film. There are Q&As, there are photographic and autograph opportunities, and one can purchase film memorabilia from the dealer tables. Today they are very popular, and very well-known entertainment entities. They are big business with huge scale events that are set up on both sides of the Atlantic, and which attract film people and customers from the same.

David Del Valle is a horror film enthusiast who, at the time I met him, had already amassed a huge collection of horror film memorabilia. Having grown up on a diet of Universal horror films such as *Dracula* and *The Mummy* with Lon Chaney and

Bela Lugosi, today, his credits and achievements include being a journalist, a radio and TV horror commentator, a film historian, an author, an uncredited actor in small film roles and a talent agent. He was inducted into the Rondo Hatton Classic Horror Awards as a Monster Kid in their Hall of Fame in 2016.

David was well-known and well-loved in his community. Friendly and affable, he held parties where he gathered people from Hammer and horror. A lot of creators and fans alike would attend his parties. Because he collected, he introduced us to his collection. One such item was a huge US 3 Sheet poster of Frankenstein. He had them all framed. He liked a drink, he was very funny, he knew his stuff about the films and the stars; indeed, his knowledge was encyclopaedic.

In January 1994, he told me about these conventions and what the opportunities might look like if I were to consider being a part of the attraction line-up. To smooth over any remaining concerns or questions I might have had, he said, 'I will come with you.' And thus, he became my agent. It was a new beginning.
He educated me as to how these events unfolded and what was required to best benefit both yourself and the quality and the smooth running of the event. I realised we had to source many photos from a wide variety of films with a wider range of poses and shots. We needed money, more specifically, change to ensure the transactions were made quickly and were not prevented because of a lack thereof. We needed a professional looking sign advertising the wares and the range of costs. We set it all up with a $10-15 range of image price points. Our first event was in Pasadena on October 16th. It was a small convention of around only 100 or so guests. Was this really what we wanted? We were all squeezed into a little conference centre and we made very little money. All our guests were very nice, and all were just casually dressed, however there were those super fans who loved to dress up as their favourite characters. But because David and I were great friends, we had a giggle. Would it get better though?

Yes. The following week on January 15th, we attended the three-day Hollywood Collectors Convention. A three-day event, it was far better and much bigger. We made a little money and it encouraged us to carry on. On 18th January, the day after the convention, we were celebrated for our efforts and successes by a huge earthquake; the biggest thus far in California. Huge mirrors crashed, there was state-wide damage, and the electricity was cut off. When power returned, we watched the outcome on a news report. As the anchor was speaking, an aftershock erupted through California again. Both news readers leapt under their desk, mid-presentation. We couldn't help laughing in the face of adversity.

In March 1994, we attended the Glamour Con. As the name suggests, involving glamour girls from the world of modelling and film, it required a whole different approach. While this was certainly amusing, and the girls were gorgeous, we admitted to ourselves that it was not quite our thing, but it was certainly an education.

Acting opportunities were again becoming a little thin on the ground. There was no work and I had been talking to Gary Goetzmann. He talked about a film called *Devil in a Blue Dress,* which was to be directed by Carl Franklin. Produced by Jonathan Demme, the film is an American neo-noir mystery thriller and starred Denzel Washington, Tom Sizemore, Jennifer Beals and Don Cheadle. The film is set in 1948 and follows a WWII veteran played by Washington who, desperate for money, assists a private investigator who is looking for a missing woman.

Gary put me in touch with Carl to be a director's assistant. It is a romantic idea. I could learn something of the behind-the-scenes aspects of film making during both production and post production. At first it was interesting working on set with Carl, but very quickly the definition of the role transferred from one of AD to PA, and then to running errands. The work ran to three months but, quite frankly, it was not the learning experience I had hoped for.

May 20th, David Del Valle and I flew to Newark on the east coast to attend the Chiller Theatre Expo. Still running to this day in New Jersey, and twice yearly, this was a fabulous event. This was a huge convention whereby over the three days, thousands of guests and celebrities attended. People showed films, live music was played and there were multitudinous Q&As. There were maybe 50 celebrities in attendance on this my first Chiller event. Friend of many years, Adam West of TV's Batman was there. So too was George Hamilton. The event took on a party atmosphere that would flow through to the evening. Some guests would dress up in a cosplay fashion. Kiss played the live music; the music was always heavy metal which was not my thing but it was always colourful.

There was even a guy who had brought with him to the event his pet bats in a cage. I had always thought bats were ugly blood sucking creatures, but not so. He brought them out of the cage, they all had names, and I loved them; they were so sweet. I was fascinated to meet the guy. And then there were other people who came with their menagerie of snakes and tarantulas. Absolutely anything could and did happen.

I have been invited to this event many times and when possible, I have done as many as I could. I missed a few due to Covid, but these are big and friendly. And the man who runs it is called Kevin Clement. We all love Kevin; he is like the king.

Conventions such as these offer regular opportunities to meet up with old friends. People with whom you have worked, other industry professionals with whom you had worked on the same film or television series but had never actually met, and people that you wish you had had the opportunity to meet but, until having attended these functions, the chance never arose. The norm at that time was to still charge $15 per still, but we went up to $20. Aside from the business of doing business, it meant fewer denominations of change would be required. They were always organised over a long weekend. You fly in on the Thursday, work Friday to Sunday, and fly out on the Monday. Sometimes they would pay for our flights, and on this occasion, they did. They are not a huge money maker, but they are always good fun. The deals to secure attendance are becoming more accommodating as the years ensure. When I fly from the UK to the US, the package includes a hotel room and sometimes a flight. To help the business venture, you would sign a number pictures for the organisers that they can sell on their own behalf. Some events offer per diems for food, like Chiller Theatre Expo.

The same year, we went to Baltimore for the Fanex, a horror convention. We met the force of nature that is Ingrid Pitt, and Veronica Carlson, James Bernard, the Hammer Horror music composer and Val Guest. This convention also introduced to us the idea that we could receive awards for our past films. And yes, I received a few of these, including one for Worst Film, for Prehistoric Women. They paid us a fee to attend this convention. The format was the same; Friday through Sunday. The Baltimore con created for us a large number of friends within the world of Hammer; there was much talking and reminiscing. This was also a break-through for us in terms of the quality of stories people told on stage. I love doing the Q&As, because it offers the possibility for a wider communication, the questions can be really interesting, they can be quite different, and they can be more involved; it gives you the opportunity to be a raconteur and to perfect that skill. The audience love hearing all the stories, and so we love telling them all the more. Unfortunately, I believe Fanex came to an end in 2005.

In September I went to another Glamour Con at the LA Sheraton. And in October 1994, I did my first James Bond convention.

In 1994, I did in total about five Conventions. In the following years I did fewer per year as we became more discerning about the subject matters and the audiences. While I lived in LA, all the conventions I attended were in the US; a few of which took me to the east coast.

## NIGHT OF THE SCARECROW

Director friend, Jeff Burr, asked me to do a film for him in the same year. Called *Night of the Scarecrow*, the premise focused on a small farming community that had just suffered a drought, and to survive, the town people make a deal with a warlock. With power and hedonism going to the warlock's head, the residents tire of his manipulations, crucify him and bury him in a stone coffin. The coffin is accidentally broken by two workers, the spirit of the warlock escapes, takes possession of a nearby scarecrow and wreaks havoc and revenge on the town. It starred John Mese and Bruce Glover and was filmed in Hanford, northern California.

It was not my favourite film as I had to be a victim and sewn up! To Jeff I said, 'You know, I am not very good being a victim.' 'Please do it for me,' he pleaded. Playing a victim for me meant crying and dying. I like being the murderess, I like being bad.

## ALONG CAME MARY

Continuing to work in areas other than acting made acting possible. I had met Mary Micucci while working at Roy's Restaurant in 1976, who was and still is a sister. She had created a catering company that had become very successful in catering to events like the Emmys, the Oscars, the Grammys and film premiere parties for the likes of *Popeye* and *Titanic*. One of her most ambitious events was the Grammys where she catered for 5000 people. Such is her reputation and success that she has been called the Queen of Themes, Madam Caterer, the Master of Special Events and the Epicurean Steven Spielberg.

The Hollywood 'A listers' pride themselves on sending gifts to all their friends and professional associates. Knowing hundreds of people makes that kindness a job of work. Today, a famous example of such Christmas gifting would be Tom Cruise, who sends cakes all around the world to his many hundreds of contacts.

Mary Micucci began a company of her own to source, pack and ship gifts for just such people for all the major holidays; Christmas, New Year, Easter and the like. She was already well-known and well respected in her catering business so perhaps she saw this business venture as a natural extension.

She called the business, Along Came Mary. A range of gifts at a range of prices would be sourced, wrapped, placed in gift basket, packed and shipped. One of her first customers was Barbara Streisand, who wanted Mary to create gift baskets with gifts ranging from $200-$1000 per gift. She might have had around 100 people to have them sent to.

So quickly had the venture escalated that for her first holiday, she had to take over an entire stage at Paramount Studios for all of the acquired gifts and the packing. She employed six of us to help out, including Candace, who was an ex-partner of Mary's at Along Came Mary. She also included Beverly Pescov, who became, and still is, a dear friend of mine. We all walked into the Paramount stage and we were aghast at the sheer size and enormity of the task that lay ahead. There were at least 40 clients who required multiple gifts to be sent to their friends and colleagues. But we did it. And she did this every year, for each of the holiday seasons in December, Christmas, New Year, Easter. Shortly after the Paramount stage experience, Mary managed to contain it in another room as opposed to in a studio. We were then hired by Candace to source the gifts. For this, we went to gift trade shows to look at anything and everything. We might have been looking for a pasta-based theme, or a bath idea.

By far the biggest such gift we ever sent was a big toy red wagon on wheels, two to three feet long and 18 inches wide. We sourced and inserted a number of other gifts to place inside the wagons, wrapped them all up, put them in the wagon, packed the whole lot up and shipped them. All beautified with bows, flowers, and wines. Only in Hollywood.

Kathleen Heinecke was an interior designer, one of my dearest sisters, and who had been my flatmate at a time when, I have to say, we certainly encouraged each other in naughtiness. I leave it to your imagination, but just to say, we were two hot girls on the prowl. These were big FUN times until she met her love, Skip Heinecke, and off she went on another adventure. Skip was a top PR executive in Hollywood. After a rocky start to my relationship with Skip because of my misdiagnosed disapproval of his suitability, I came to love him dearly and still do, to this day. They moved to Bangkok as his brother, Bill, and wife Kathy, lived and worked there. Bill's company, Minor International, is an umbrella company that has businesses in hospitality, hotels, restaurants and lifestyle brands. Skip went to work with Bill. Kathleen, my brilliant friend, learned Thai and also worked for Bill designing various interiors and particularly a boat fitted out as a sailing hotel.

For some of these ventures, she wanted Californian memorabilia and subsequent to a conversation, I became her buyer. I travelled all over California and 11 bags later, I got on a flight to Bangkok and ended up staying for six weeks as her assistant designer. At this time, another great friend, Betty Marvin, ex-wife to Lee Marvin, arrived in Bangkok as part of her round the world trip. She and I took off to Koh Samui. We rented a little beach hut for $20, put on our swimsuits for the days, sarongs at night, and had the most delicious five days, especially because we met this lovely German couple who owned a small hotel a few foot steps down the beach from us. Hearing Nina Simone wafting in the breeze, we were drawn to their pagoda. Introducing ourselves, this was followed by margaritas, hashish, and great food. Magical.

The six weeks with Kathleen and Skip, and also getting to know Bill and Kathy, was very special. The next year, she shipped me in again with more memorabilia that I had been tasked to source. Bliss. How lucky was I? They now live in Ireland and, as I am included in their Irish tribes, I regularly visit them.

## ▊ RANCHO MONTE ALEGRE

Around 1976, Michael Taylor met Ray Underwood, an actor, poet, singer, and his soulmate, Julianna Wooton, an actress. Michael and Ray began a passionate affair. Ray introduced us to his brother Val, a classic pianist whose forte was Chopin. Needless to say, I fell in love with the brothers and Julianna.

Val moved from LA to a ranch in Carpenteria. The ranch was called Rancho Monte Alegre. Michael moved to New York to continue work as a top model and to write his book titled, Male Model. Ray and I became inseparable and began to make endless weekend trips to see Val in Carpenteria.

Rancho Monte Alegre is a 3500-acre avocado and lemon farm in the Carpenteria foothills. There were water falls, swimming pools, and mountains that backed on to the foothills. The land used to host a Chumash Indian Village in the 1600s and which leant a certain history to the ranch. It was by far the biggest ranch in that area.

On one of these weekends, we heard about a Chumash pow wow that was to be held in the Santa Inez valley, and which was open to the public. Ray and I leaped in my car and off we went in great excitement. Upon arrival, we joined the other people who had signed up in the afternoon. We went to the top of the mountain where, at that moment, the Indians were building a huge round fire pit. Some, but not all of the Indians were in ceremonial outfits. In a circle around the fire pit, they had placed some straw bales for us to sit on.

Sunset arrived, and it was a lovely evening. One of the Indians lit the fire; it was huge. We were all given something to eat, beans and rice. The meal was delicious and the evening was about to begin. The drums were brought out, all of different sizes, two big drums, a couple of hand-sized ones, some stand-up ones; in all about 20. The drumming and the chanting began, and we are completely blown away by it all. Twilight arrived and the excitement grew.

One thing that permeated but did not spoil the evening was the catastrophic affect that the beans had on us all. There was quite a lot of passing of air and without the clearing effects of a light breeze, it was very smelly. Everyone conspired to ignore it, but we began to giggle. The dancing commenced and the young son of the chief, himself in full Indian garb, came to me, offered me his hand, and asked me to dance. 'This is happening to me!' I am in heaven. While all this was happening, down in the valley, the Indians had made a sweat lodge. Shaped like a dome and with a fire in the middle of it, they had draped carpets over a frame of wood and to keep the heat in, they used another carpet for the door.

After the dancing had finished, with the others, Ray and I went down to the valley to the sweat lodge. We had to wait a while as the Indians were not quite ready. We all sat on the ground. There were no seats or chairs. We were with 10 or so other people. We did not know any of them. We were directed to remove our clothes, all of them. We were completely naked. Once the Indians were ready, we were invited into the carpet covered dome through the small doorway. Inside there was a circle of bales and again, we all sat facing each other. The leader chanted to the great spirit, he said prayers, and he passed a peace pipe around the circle. We were all sweating profusely, it was pouring off us all. Some people couldn't take it and left. Not Ray and I. We were determined to see this through for what it was. We had sat in the smoky heat for perhaps an hour when something very magical happened. We had got to a point when we felt we couldn't take it any more even though we wanted to keep going, and quite magically, something lifted us and our hearts opened; we felt a joy through a purification of our spirits. Was it just the pipe with the herbs that helped us get there?

It was not comfortable sitting on the straw bales, with our legs together, not crossed; you could not move around. But once you had got past the discomfort zone, there was something freeing about being naked in the company of all these

163

male and female strangers. At the end of the session, those that were left went outside. It was noticeably cooler outside at 2am. The Indians had built a huge wooden vat which they filled with ice cold water. A dip in that and the cleansing was complete.

We all then went back up to the top and put our clothes on. The fire was still burning so we lay on the ground and went to sleep. I woke up and the first thing I saw was an Indian in full out outfit stoking the fire. He looked like something out of a painting. I wrapped myself in a fur coat and welcomed in the new day. I sat in wonder on the mountain plateau and considered the surroundings in which it had all happened. The trees and the mountains around me, I went through all the mental images I had as the experience had unfolded from the afternoon, from twilight, to sunset and to sunrise.

We went down the mountain for something to eat after which we had a full medicine gathering where to the accompaniment of the drums, the chief talked of the spiritual life. I can't tell you all the words he used, but we were immersed; it was a moment of wonder, and amusement, and spirituality. And we fully understood everything he said, everything he meant and everything about his belief system. I think after all the singing, the dancing, the drumming, and the sweat lodge, we had been transported to a place where we were ready to hear this, and accept it, their words.

The talk ended, there were a lot of heartfelt thank yous, and we got in our car and left. Our jaws had dropped. Ray and I didn't really talk on the way home other than some random recollecting, 'And then there was that moment. How did you feel about that?' Otherwise, we were very quiet and reflective. We had been allowed into something that the Indian tribes do not usually allow outside of their fraternity. But for some reason, this had been opened for the public. We had no idea why. But it was beyond our dreams and expectations.

This became one of the most important experiences of my life, something that had deeply touched me and that I understood I would never able to do again. As well as instilling my love of Indian people and of drumming, I would forever and thereafter pray to the Great Spirit, the lives in all of creation, in trees, in flowers, and in animals. And not God. I had never followed my mother's path in religion and maybe because I had always thought, 'it' was much more than just a god. To cleanse yourself, to heal yourself, to recognise the power within yourself and to accept the earth and the planet and the Great Spirit; this is what to my mind religion should be about. I never tried to replicate the sweat lodge, but I adopted the idea of the Great Spirit. I say my prayers all the time, but not to God, to everything; the flowers and the trees.

Free again in the Rancho Monte Alegre

Over the course of Val's living in the Ranch, he had become great friends with the two families who owned the Ranch and which gave him great freedom of the entire property. There were two main houses with guest houses, and five other old California style cottages that housed long-term renters. When a cottage became available, Val called a friend to inform him of its vacancy. He would then move in. He continued to do this until all our friends occupied all the cottages and thence a community of what was described as, Those Bohemians, was formed. We all joined forces to nurture the beautiful tropical gardens that surrounded every cottage. We dined at each other's houses, sang, danced, drummed, hiked into the hills, dipped in the pools and waterfalls. One of the plateaus we walked to, to take in the views, must have been used as a cooking area as a huge bowl had been dug, probably for a fire pit. This was called Indian Rock.

165

Although the ranch was called Rancho Monte Alegre, we decided to rename it as our little dukedom, called the Duchy of Dragonia, as named after a magnificent 200-year-old Dragon tree that greeted you as you entered through the gates to the Ranch. Every one of us who lived on the Duchy got a title. Val of course was the Duke and I became Duchess of Dragonia. Chris Harrington is the Earl. His husband, Jacques Pryor, is a Hawaiian Royal (he was born on Maui), Alli Nui. Julianna Wooton, now Shoba Satya, and with her partner, Hania Cerrnerazzo, are the countesses. And Jeanine Altmeyer, a Wagner opera singer, is the Principessa.

Only friends who slept over were given a title. However, visiting friends were allowed to be Lords and Ladies. 'My darling Duke', 'My dearest Duchess', would be heard around the houses. To this day, we still address each other by our titles; we invented Fun, and the fun is never ending. Over the years, my Duchy has flown me to various places which included Las Vegas, Hawaii, Puerto Rico and Sicily for my 75th birthday. In Sicily, we rented a huge historic villa with four separate cottages, which also included a delightful couple, who cooked delicious meals and took care of all our needs. They also became part of my birthday celebrations.

The birthday dinner was a delicious three-course sit down affair on one of the terraces, surrounded by seven gorgeous boys in full toga and wig costumes. An evening never to be forgotten. In fact, the entire week had to be one of the most extraordinary events in my life. We went on daily jaunts all over Sicily and had a lunch in Taormina at the Penis Café. Everything is literally in the shape of a penis; the furniture, chairs, door knobs, crockery, taps, everything. And actually, it was quite artistic. As you can imagine, everything was fondled together with a great deal of laughter.

Val's mother was a videographer and photographer. Val himself was a concert pianist, a voice coach for opera singers, a music teacher and he was also the head of Hawaiian Performing Arts Festival, a Festival that continues to today to bring young musicians together from all over the world to perform with professional musicians to play anything from classical music to musical theatre.

Val was particularly superb at playing the music of Frédéric Chopin. He could play it drunk, tired, asleep, you name it. He was by then used to putting on concerts and shows in music halls and he suggested we all, our little community, should create a Chopin Festival and perform it in our neighbouring town of Santa Barbara. He involved us all. He played the Chopin pieces and actor friends read letters written by characters in Chopin's life creating his biography on stage.

166

The Duke and Duchess of Dragonia. Val and Martine

My role was to play the writer, Dupin Dudevant, who cross dressed and published her novels under the pseudonym, George Sand, and with whom Chopin had a much-romanticised relationship. I played the role as cross dressed and in male clothes. We performed over several nights to about 100 people and it was directed by Ray and photographed by Rilla Belle, Val and Ray's mother.

I had discovered drumming in Jamaica and had played them while I was in Death Valley. I was also a dancer. When I was in Death Valley, I had discovered an Indian made drum, a little one and which had been beautifully painted. It made a lovely sound. It had followed me around and it came with me to the Ranch. When we had picnics in the meadow, I brought it with me and started playing it as if I had played my whole life. It created a beautiful sound and the others in our group started singing and chanting that connected entirely to the area of the world in which we were habiting. The enthusiasm for drumming took on a life force of its own whereby to later picnics, everyone had to bring a drum. Indian drumming is something whereby there was a point when the rhythm kind of got into your body, and you just went into it. Something happened to you. I led many a drumming session, but I had never specifically learned it or was taught it; I just felt it. I would drum to such a degree that I would experience an almost electric feeling. When it worked, you felt committed to it; it was so exhilarating.

We would take the drums up to Indian Rock and drum all night long; it was another amazing feeling that everyone experienced. A weird thing was, if professionally trained musicians got involved with us in the drumming, it actually took them a while to flow into mood. They were thinking of a beat, but no, the thing was to embrace what you felt at that moment. And when they got it, they too contributed to a wonderful sound. And then you got to a crescendo, and your hair stood up; so exciting. I found drumming to be a wonderful way of getting in touch with your soul. It was the same with dancing. Like Michael Jackson, he was someone who could not, not dance. It was a happy curse; drumming and dancing were my curses which I embraced fully and did not care what people thought.

Many years later when back living in London, I had gone to the Reading Rock Festival. I found a drum and bought it. I saw this group of about 20 people sitting in a circle drumming. My heart began to pound. I joined them and they let me join in. It was like surfing where if you managed to hit the wave just right, the joy is incomparable. This was the same kind of joy. In the middle of the circle, there was a little platform. I was dressed in cowboy boots, a skirt and a shirt; your standard bohemian festival outfit. I put my drum down and stepped on to the platform. I started to dance, I chanted, I surrendered to the trance, the drummers beat faster, the sweat was pouring off my body, my hair was flying everywhere, I was now controlled by the beat of the drums, I could not stop, I was exhausted but there was no letting go, they needed to stop beating the drums because I could not stop. 'You need to stop now,' I cried. The exhaustion was total, the immersion was complete and finally, the drummers finally slowed down, they brought me back to earth, and they stopped.

## ■ RESTAURANT

It was 1997, I had by then moved to the Rancho Monte Alegre and the calls for acting seemed not to be so frequent. They say an actor never really retires; it is just that the telephone stops ringing. Well, for the past year it had been exactly like that. The income generated from attending the conventions was providing very nicely, as David Del Valle and I jointly navigated the options and returns from the many convention variants.

When my agent did call, it was for one or two minor scenes. The last straw landed thuddingly on my back when I was put up for the US TV series, *Falcon Crest*. I was up against Sarah Douglas, an actress up against whom I already been when casting was looking for someone to play Ursa in Christopher Reeves' *Superman 1* and *Superman 2*. She had pipped me to that role. And she pipped me again to *Falcon Crest*. Sarah did 51 episodes as 'Pamela Lynch' between 1983 and 1985 and then left the show. When the writers wanted for reasons best known to themselves to make the character return, they did so with me and explained the different actors away with the daytime-soap-sensibilities of plastic surgery.

That was it. That was the last thing I did. I had lost the passion, really. I thought, believed and decided, I do not need to go begging for two scenes in anything. I had been in films; I had been the named guest star in high profile television series. I said to my agent, 'Look, I can't do this anymore.' I cut it off; I had picked myself up once too many times. As an actor who had put myself through that journey, as any actor who today puts themselves continually through that journey, and who understands the never-ending fight to be recognised, realised and properly featured based maybe only on one's long-term learning of the craft and the industry, that is what I, we, all of us subscribe ourselves to doing.

Or, in my case, and as of this moment, had subscribed myself to doing. To have been so passionate about acting, but to then also to have serially suborned my soul for the next magical and meaningful part only to have ultimately withstood the equally serial rejection, the steely aspect of old within me had had enough.

I became happily retired. That was that. Enough.

I had met Ellen Sherman in Jamaica through good friends Chris Blackwell and Dickie Jobson. She had been working in New York for NBC on documentaries and before that had been an actress. She suggested that I get in touch with Stefanie Bennett, an investor who, two years previously, had opened up a successful restaurant in LA called The Newsroom. She was considering opening a café in Carpenteria. Ellen did tell me that Stephanie was quite tricky, but that equally she was very professional and felt that she and I would get on.

The Newsroom restaurant offered everything; breakfast, lunch and dinner. She knew everything about restaurants, I loved food and cooking, we had the meeting and we clicked. We agreed that the new café would offer only lunch fare and that I would be the manager of the site. We went to The Newsroom to see their operation and to discuss how to go about setting it up.

Returning to Carpenteria, we found a place on the main street, 865 Linden Avenue. It was sat next to a nursery for plants and flowers, the café windows looked out on to the flowers. The café site needed some work so we arranged for some meetings with a range of architects and builders. Stefanie would invest money in the project; my investment would be my time as the manager for a 15% of the takings.

Stefanie's strength was not in creating and maintaining relationships with people. It is a strength of mine and very quickly I became the front woman for the kitchen and food suppliers and to encourage them to give us a line of credit. Protect the cash flow. The builders came in and I motivated a number of my friends to help. It all required a lot of organisation.

I realised that we did not have a huge financial backing but, we were only focusing on lunch so we should manage. We had some lovely ideas. We wanted to use organic produce; we found some great bread people. We went to the Rose Bowl Flea Market in Pasadena. We found antique chairs and tables and painted them all different colours to make the environment warm and fun. As Stefanie was British, we designed the menu to focus on English mains and desserts with custard.
It was all taking shape. The stoves and fridges arrived and the café was designed for a 50-seat capacity. We set up the demos and taster sessions and on June 8th, we signed all the contracts and engaged a head chef and head waitress.

We named it the Delilah Café and confirmed an opening date of the July 5th.

And on June 27th, Stefanie announced that she and her husband would be going on a safari to Africa to return on July 10th.

I was shocked. I coerced my friends to come in to work and help. We opened on July 5th and of course, everything went badly. The oven didn't work properly, the cash register broke down, and the chef was comparatively new to the demands and excitement of an opening day. It was a day of disasters. We managed to put the food out and against all odds, it was a success.

Stephanie returned from Africa on July 10th and her latest announcement was that she had decided we now needed to offer dinner. We had barely recovered from the opening and we were looking to settle into a rhythm and routine to build our success. We had also designed the kitchen around a lunch only offering. We did not have enough fridges and stoves for all the different ingredients and drinks. I went back to my suppliers to ask another of this and that. We got it, and we installed it. The lunch menu was only 11.30 to 4pm. The dinners were good, the food was really good. People were laughing and people were talking. I did my Hellos and created some lovely relationships with the staff, the suppliers and the customers. The restaurant had a nice ambience, and the reviews were good; excellent in fact. But I was working until 4am.

Stefanie's involvement with the restaurant was minimal. She rarely visited and had nothing to do with the staff. And whenever she did turn up, there was always an announcement, like, 'We should now do breakfast.'

We stayed with the English foods theme and streamlined the menus to afford the best chance of moving from one time of the day to the next.

Breakfast was mostly full English, which, while it sounds obvious, is the most difficult dish to create, as it is all about timing the cooking of the various ingredients. Nothing can be pre-cooked. We also offered great toast. Americans were bad at toast; it always came out floppy. This was important for a good breakfast

Lunch was Paninis, sandwiches and salads with chicken, fish, ham and steak. Dinner, we offered fish and vegies, stews and shepherds' pie, which was a huge hit. And for desserts, apple crumble and pear crumble with custard. People loved it; very simple, very tasty.

But we were over-stretching ourselves. We had never really had the time to consolidate our position before leaping into the next venture. As each new venture was implemented, an extra level of financial investment was required but that which never came. This meant we had to self-finance each new strand of the operation. Cash flow is king, but in November, the impending crisis hit us. We could not pay our suppliers. I had paid my waitresses and chefs first. My suppliers came second, until they couldn't, and I came last. The reality of that last statement is that I had not taken a salary for myself since after the very first month, and we had been in business for almost a year and open for five months.

Delilah Cafe

It is a standard thing within start-ups and new companies for the investors to not take money out of the business before there is profit and cash flow. As mentioned above, my 'investment' for the 15% commission was my managerial time, and Stefanie's was cash. Stefanie too had not taken money from the business, but she had other means of support. We had needed another investor or further investment.

I had been surprised by the constant upping of the ante, which led to always needing more equipment. My practicality and organisational abilities and my common sense played to get it all off the ground. Perhaps I should have pushed back on the demands to upscale. My staff was also not top notch. We couldn't afford to hire seasoned chefs and waiters, so I elected to hire young people who had come straight out of colleges or schools that focused on teaching the restaurant business. But they had never really worked, they were still just students. Our chef was quite good, but he had an affair with Stefanie's daughter with distracting results.

I had fully committed to making the restaurant work, I had hoped all was going to be ok, but I realised I was never going to be paid. I had also been falling behind in paying for the food and the farmers. My stupidity. Stephanie had no option but to close the restaurant and so it was the end of Delilah Café.

Stefanie and I never had arguments; we probably did not communicate enough with each other to lead to such issues. We had enjoyed putting the restaurant together, Stefanie and I. It had been exciting and fun, and we really did do a good job in putting it together. I think we managed to pay off some of them. The food people had anyway stopped delivering. I worked out I was owed about $10k but there was nothing I could do. I could not go to small claims court as it would have taken me years to resolve. It had been my responsibility and thus, it was my fault. It had been a hard lesson.

I was living at the ranch and I related the news to my Duchy. Of course they were concerned for my welfare, but they were also aware that as a group, we had leant to the restaurant various utensils and paintings to mitigate some of the initial set-up costs. 'Listen, if this is the situation now, we are going in there at midnight to take everything back.' My gang drove into Carpenteria at midnight to take everything back and that is what we did. And then we shut the door.
I never spoke to Stefanie again.

On 29th Dec, I flew to London to be with mummy and my sister. I told them the sad tale of the restaurant and Laurellie said that if I decided to return to London, she would be happy to have me stay with her. I saw some friends like Jeremy Clyde. I had been subsisting on three to four hours' sleep a night for the last year. I was thin, drawn and in much need of a rest.

I travelled back to Carpenteria on 26th Jan 1998. I went for walks every day on the ranch and one morning I stopped and asked the universe, 'What do I do now?' And suddenly, as if there was a voice around me, I heard, 'You have to be with your family.' I hadn't been working as an actress, the restaurant had closed, I didn't want to leave my friends but I realised that was exactly what I had to do. I just howled until there were no tears left to cry. I had to go back to London. My mind was made up, the decision was made. It was Feb 28th.

I began to sell everything, my furniture, my car, everything. On March 7th, my friends decided to throw a funding and farewell party for me. It sounded awful. 'You can't do that,' I remonstrated. 'You are the Duchess, and the Duchess needs her shekels. We must all pay our taxes to the Duchess.' Christopher Harrington, the Earl of our group, set it all up. And he did it very well; the party was wonderful; people were incredibly generous. It became a good send off.

On 12th March 1998, I caught the red-eye to London, and to what would become my new life.

# 11

## 1998-2024

# LONDON, NEW BEGINNINGS

---

■ **FRANCINE WINHAM**

Upon my return to England, I needed to hook up with as many of my old friends as possible. One such was Francine Winham, the performer, artist, and jazz photographer that I had first met and shared a house with in London in the 1960s.

Francine was the richest bohemian I ever knew. She had been born into the family of a self-made property tycoon who, during the war, had moved the family to the comparative safety of Colorado. Returning to the UK, she had been sent to the Mitford-Colmer Seminary for Young Ladies in Belgravia; a sort of finishing school for debutants whose paths would lead to the very best of husbands and all that that would bring with it. But Francine's ideas followed different paths when she first heard Boogie Woogie being played on an old piano.

It was then that we met each other because her sister, Josephine, and her husband were great friends with Chris Blackwell. Francine then became part of the Connaught Square gang, as she was having an affair with Winston Stona, an actor who was also living in the house.

At a certain moment, Chris offered her a job to work with him in Island Records. Francine's father then gave her a Rolliflex camera and she started to photograph everything. She became a photographer. Chris suggested that she should photograph the record covers. Now a photographer with a portfolio, she moved to New York in 1963 and started photographing all the jazz performers such as Miles Davis, John Coltrane and Nina Simone. She sold her photography to all the music and entertainment magazines.

Francine returned to London in 1967 where she later joined the Woman's Film Group and where her unconventional style of photography leant itself naturally into film making. She made a short film with Judy Geeson. The fact was that Francine was just one of these multitalented individuals that could turn their hand to anything creative, their self-belief powering them through to success on the other side. She was a photographer, a screenwriter, a jazz and opera singer, a political activist, and an art collector.

Francine and I had a reunion on 17th April 1998 and I was invited to Joldwynds, a 1930s Grade II listed art deco house which sits in the Surrey Hills, and had, through Francine, already gained a reputation for being a central hub for the gathering of artists, authors, concerts, filming, retreats and charitable events.

When I arrived at Joldwynds, already present were Diana 'Dee Dee' Glass, an American born documentary film maker, Joan Safran, an American philosophy teacher and Marxist, Donatella Moores, the Littlewoods heiress, Gareth Humphreys, her ex-partner but who still managed her estates and worked as a screenwriter for Peter Morgan, Gareth's wife, Catherine Doran, and Brenda Cole, Francine's housekeeper and cook of many decades, who literally managed the whole property.

Francine had two grand pianos in the house on which she and Gareth would play jazz. 'Roses', my alter ego, also played her symphonies with pride and joy. No one believed I had never had a lesson.

When Francine was in New York photographing, she had taken and had brought back with her some incredible jazz photography. She gifted me a Nina Simone photo which to this day hangs with pride on my wall. Whenever I see her lighting, her brilliance, it makes my heart glow with great love.

Francine organised concerts at her house, 'cos she could afford to.' She would sing her opera songs and I had a light bulb moment. I thought, her voice could use some work; she has to meet Val, my Duke in Carpenteria at the Ranch. He is a brilliant voice coach and I just knew they would like each other. He flew over from Carpenteria, they met, they connect, and together they started to organise concerts at Joldwynds where everyone got involved and when Australian opera singer and star, Jennifer McGregor, performed at the house. The first time she sang at their concert, we heard the beauty of her voice and tears were running down our faces.

Jazz and Opera singing master classes were given at Joldwynds that led to Val coming back and forth from Carpenteria. I too joined the classes. With all the artistic and creative people always milling around at Joldwynds, Francine would encourage you or indeed boss you around to become involved and to stretch yourself. 'You've got to do it. You've got to sing. You have to.' On one of these weekend classes, she had become friends with a renowned British jazz singer, pianist and composer, Liane Carroll, and invited her to give a master class at Joldwynds. She was an inspiring teacher who accompanied us on the piano. She was also very funny and it was a truly joyous experience.

The drums came to Joldwynds. New Year was a favourite of everyone at the house, a party where we also had a firework display and a feast for 10-14 people, and I led everyone in drumming. We could be as loud as we wanted to be, as there was no one around.

Francine was the definition of generosity. She insisted I join her in her singing class that was held in Barnes and led by Shireen Francis, a Jamaican jazz singer. 'You have to join. I will pay for it.' It was a 12-week class and at the end, we all had to perform at the very well-known jazz venue, the Bull's Head. We had three songs each. Mum and friends came to see us. It was scary, but very exciting, and a real joy.

Francine invited Mum to Joldwynds after Laurellie died and Mum fell in love with the house and the atmosphere. If she ever found out I went to Joldwynds alone, there would be trouble. I had to sneak away. Even at 100 years of age, she was singing and drumming with everyone. Everyone adored May. If I was going to the house, 'Is May coming,' I would be asked. Mum was so proud. She had taken piano lessons in the past so she could play. When Francine heard this, she said, 'You have to keep playing.' 'But I don't have a piano.' Francine told me, 'Go find a piano and let me know where it is and how much it is. She has to have a piano.'

This was just like Francine; when she had an idea, she did it. She was beyond generous. We had incredible meals there too. We all brought supplies. Whenever

Brenda was not there, one of us would take over. I went for long weekends, probably once or twice a month; Christmas and NY, sometimes Easter, people's birthdays. There was always an excuse to go there. And on one occasion, we very nearly didn't get there.

Dec 25 2012, Mum and I had been invited for Christmas. Staying for several days, we had loaded the car with luggage and presents for everyone. It had been raining heavily the day before. Not too far from Joldwynds there was a sizeable dip in the road that had filled with water. Not thinking, not realising and not questioning myself just how deep the water might have been, I drove straight on. And stopped. Yup, I had made a mistake. The engine gave out. The water quickly found its way into the car and up to our knees. There was no one obviously around. This was the country, full of countryside and no people. We hesitated to open the door as the water would rush in. But, what do we do? We figured I at least had better get out and of course, the water rushed in. All the presents began to float in the back seat. The suitcases were in the trunk.

Looking around at our plight, we noticed a guy standing at the top of a little hill who had got out of his car and had been taking photos of us. He wore a coat and a flat cap. He seemed not to have realised that there had been anyone in our car. I waved to him, beckoning him to come down. Stating the obvious and the evident, I said, 'We can't move. Would you have any idea what I can do. My mother cannot move as she is 90 years old.'

He took off his coat and hat, stripped down to his knickers, and walked into water, barefoot and up to his knees. The country road was full of pebbles and rocks. 'Oh my God, I am so sorry,' I offered. He opened the door, lifted Mum out of the car and carried her up to the top of the hill. We saw some houses. The residents saw us and came out to offer their news. 'Someone did that exact same thing only a few hours ago,' they informed. Great, I thought. Safety in numbers of stupidity. They called the police and fire brigade. Flat cap was called Paul Wells and he had become very emotional. Tears had formed in his eyes and were falling down his cheeks. Now what? He had just come from his local church. He choked, 'I feel like I have 'been sent' to take care of you.'

The fire brigade arrived, handsome guys, three to four of them. They clambered into waterproof overalls and began to collect the floating presents and the suitcases from their watery demise. The car could not be moved or towed until the water had dissipated. Our heroic angel told us he would take us to wherever we were going. Everything was stacked in his car and we continued our journey. But since the normal, tried and tested way had been blocked, an alternate route had to be found. It was not easy. We needed to find a phone. My mobile phone hadn't died along with everything else, but there was no signal. We had now missed lunch at Joldwynds. We had no idea where we were. We found someone with a phone, and called Joldwynds to speak to someone who knew the area and could direct our hero in his car.

We finally arrived at Joldwynds and our winged saviour was stunned by the house and was ushered into the dining room where everyone was still gathered around the table. They all welcomed him and thanked him and asked him many questions while Mum and I went off to change out of our wet clothes. On our return, Brenda served the three of us with one of her delicious Christmas dinners, after which we hugged our hero and waved him off. Darling Francine was a constant in my life until the day she died on 29th December 2013.

After this, the era of debating, music, and everything ended at Joldwynds. The house was left to her beloved nieces, but it was now rented out as a film venue. It is huge, and very expensive to keep up, so at least it is still there, even if the creative hub has found a new home elsewhere and under someone else's care and love. It really was a beautiful building that through Francine was filled with incredible events and joy.

And Francine was at the epicentre of it all. We miss her terribly.

## ■ FLORENCE

In October 2001, Val's very good friends, a Swedish couple called Steaffan and Margareta Encrantz, were throwing themselves a party. Ostensibly it was a 50th birthday party thrown by Margareta for Steaffan, but otherwise it was an opportunity to gather a number of their good friends from around the world that they had not seen for a while. There were 50 guests, of whom we were four; Val, me and Chris and his then boyfriend, later husband, Jacques. Chris was a realtor and Jacques was a Hawaiian singer who, through his brother's school boy friendship with Barack Obama, had sung at the White House. We were all graduates of the Rancho Monte Alegre and as Val had been voice coaching Margareta in opera singing, and as she was also involved with Val in the Hawaiian Performance Arts Festival, and as she had been a long term and frequent visitor to the Ranch, we were invited to the 50th.

Steaffan and Margareta decided to hold the event in Florence. They had booked the five-star Excelsior Hotel that sits on the banks of the Arno River. However, weeks before the event, we had to give our measurements. We were to be fitted for renaissance style costumes.

When we arrived at hotel, the costumes were there and ready. There were also a few seamstresses available and on hand in case there was a need to fine-tune the fit. Everyone had been flown in from different parts of the world and, through the afternoon, everyone dressed in their costumes and the ladies were given headdresses and were fully made-up. In the evening, we descended for cocktails in the lounge. In the same way as a suit makes a man consider his posture and shoulders, so too were the costumes making everyone play up the royalty.

We were invited out to the piazza in front of the hotel and alongside the Arno, and we were greeted by a huge line of drummers, also in costume. Waving flags, they greeted us with a rendition of powerful drumming. The early evening was beautiful, the setting sun glistened along the length of the Arno; it was like something straight out of a film. We were in awe of the beauty.

Duchy treated as deserved in Florence

After drums and flags, we were then led east along the river to the Palazzo Corsini, a 17th century palace that had been appropriated by the Italian banking and political dynasty family, the House of the Medicis. The gates opened to the front of the palace and in the courtyard area, acrobats, fire eaters, stilt walkers, drummers and fireworks all worked in unison to light up the twilight sky. We sat on gold chairs to watch. It was all out of a Shakespeare film.

We were then taken into the castle's ballroom for dinner that began with a series of speeches and toasts before we consumed the lovely food. It was followed by music and dancing, the lovely costumes conspiring to keep us in our 17th century royal minds.

The following morning, a little worse for wear, we were taken on a tour of Florence. Little busses took us to a number of places of interest. I had never been to Florence before and it was as stunning as all the people had told me it was. We stopped off at various buildings and museums; the Uffizi Art Gallery being one. The day's sun again accentuated the beauty of the city. We walked over the nearby Ponte Vecchio, the beautiful covered stone bridge that spans the Arno at its narrowest point. Today lined with jeweller and art dealer shops, when it was built in the Roman times, the shops were occupied by the farmers, tanners and butchers to sell their wares.

We returned to the Excelsior for a rest and to prepare for that evening's soiree. This time dressed in evening wear, we were taken to the Grand Hotel Adriatico across the piazza from the Excelsior.

There were more toasts and then the American soprano opera singer, Jeannine Altmeyer, and also one of our Ranch opera singers, sang an aria for them. Then Margareta sang an opera for them. To say this was undoubtedly one of the most amazing happenings that I have ever experienced would be to admit a huge understatement. Of the course, the generosity exemplified by Steaffan and Margareta Encrantz was on a whole other level but so too was the thinking, design and creation of this two-day event. They now live in San Francisco and Val flies in regularly from his home in Hawaii to visit them.

The day after the birthday celebrations, all four of us hired a car and disappeared off to another Italian adventure.

181

## ■ SISTER

I moved in with Laurellie on March 13th. It was a Friday, the Ides of March. She lived in a flat on Claverton Street in Pimlico, and both Laurellie and Mum were there, waiting for me. It was a lovely reunion; now it was the time to really enjoy each other's company. It was the prodigal return of their sister and daughter.

By now, the flat was paid for by a housing association. As she was always in and out of hospital, as she had been sectioned, as the massive drugs and the electric treatment had affected her, there was no way she would ever be able to work again. She had been a nurse caring for others, and now she was on disability benefits and being cared by others.

My sister and I were very close until I left for LA in 1974 and when she became unwell. Whenever I could though, I would fly to London to see her. But when she was down, I would be the evil person. Maybe what could trigger some of that was my lifestyle. She never got into the sex, drugs and rock 'n' roll in the way I did and that could have been a source of ire. All we would have to do was to look at each other and that would be enough to set us off, which made it all the more generous and kind of her to invite me to stay with her. It became an opportunity to rebuild our relationship at a time of her illness, which she had said, 'I would not wish on my worst enemy.'

Our relationship was rekindled. It became to be a lovely time that would be filled with walks in Battersea Park and along the River Thames. She and I had some amazing friends who were very close to her when she had been out of hospital for longer periods. Not having had, but wanting children, she became a surrogate mother to her friends' children. Maybe her relationships were even more special because they had gone through so many of her times with her. They were very loyal to her. Our many mutual friends included Elsa and Roderick Peters, Esther Anderson, Francine Wenham, Judy Geeson, Gabriella Lucidi and Alibe Parsons, all of whom were very supportive to Laurellie.

I started to look for a flat. She said, 'If it is not good enough, don't take it. I will tell you when it is right.' She was quite nicely bossy about it. 'If it is not right, stay with me long as it takes.' She came with me to see them, and we would both look at each other in disbelief at what was offered. It was hilarious. I was looking for something in a village atmosphere, possibly Battersea, something that would have a garden. I was lucky to have her with me, as she spotted things that needed attention and that would need to be considered before she would offer me her approval.

It was a happy family again and it confirmed my decision to be in London with them both.

In July 2000, she had another episode which led to her being hospitalised again. The medicines that were used to control bipolar disorder balance the mind for a period, but it also completely dulls the senses. What this infers is that as soon as one finds balance, you then need to come off the meds to get a sense of being alive and vital. But then of course, it causes havoc for the balance. She stayed in hospital for two months.

The next episode occurred in 2001 where, again, she was hospitalised for two months. Sweetness to chaos and back to sweetness again. That year, I had found my new home and I entertained my family with Christmas at Beswicke's. Everyone had their own room; there was much eating and lots of conviviality. On Christmas morning, the three of snuggled up in bed for a photograph. Everyone was very happy and Laurellie was particularly so. This coincided at a time where she had peace and harmony, and we loved her for it. She was at one of the happiest moments of her life.

Three Beswicks in bed for the last Christmas before Laurellie passed

On 3rd January 2002, we got a call to say that Laurellie had been hit by a bus. The police told us that she had been taken to King's College hospital. Laurellie was in a coma. We were shattered and shocked by this news. The doctor had operated on her for a brain-related injury. We visited every day hoping she would pull through; that our presence, our voices, and our touch would awaken her senses to inspire a return to the world, to be with her family and to be loved.

On January 17th, Laurellie died. Mum and I were of course deeply sad, but at the same time a part of us understood that perhaps, she just did not want to be around any longer.

Quite bizarrely, on what became Laurellie's last day, Mum and I visited the hospital chapel. We talked to the lady reverend about our current situation and Mum asked her, 'Would she come with us to see Laurellie?' We had no idea that this was going to be the last time we would see Laurellie, but the reverend was with us. It seemed fitting.

We attended the inquest and we heard a witness relate her witnessing of Laurellie's accident. She said, 'I shouted to warn her, but I thought she must have been deaf.' This became the defining moment that confirmed that which Mum and I had long suspected. It was definitely suicide. I had experienced things with Laurellie before which had made me question whether she had had suicidal tendencies. When she crossed the road, she seemed not always to look left and right. She just stepped into the road in a quite imperious fashion. I would ask what she thought she was doing but she would just say, 'Don't worry, they will just stop for me.' It would freak me out. And now, it had become obvious that she had been playing with the idea for some time.

Mum and I had to accept Laurellie's desire to end her life. It was deeply sad, and I was so glad to be back in London and to be with Mum.

Then there was the funeral. Francine offered her house in St John's Wood and also arranged a limousine for Mum and I to go to the crematorium. Dee Dee, Joan and Donatella took over and helped to organise the catering for the celebration. There were tears and stories, and just writing this brings it all back to me; I am tearing up again. The gathering all knew Laurellie so well and were able to relate the funniest stories about her. And there were many.

The joy of the funeral subsided into the reality of what we wanted to do with her. She had been cremated but I, or we, decided that we did not want to bury her. And I wanted to get a bench for her. I looked into it, and found I couldn't afford it. I issued a note to my people, informing of what we hoped to do for Laurellie; everyone came through. We ordered a bench. Her friends knew her as the Empress of Pimlico. We had a brass plaque engraved to say as much and we had it placed in Battersea Park; her favourite park and her favourite place right near to the Pagoda. We scattered her ashes in the Thames. 'Fly away my darling.' It turned out to be a really lovely moment; we drank champagne to her.

It was when we cleared out her flat that it hit the both of us in the solar plexus. Her clothes, the smells of her, the bits of her life; to touch the artefacts of life when that life has moved on was impossibly moving. The howls of sorrow poured forth. We got ourselves together. We loved her so dearly, but it was so hard to watch this brilliant mind be put in that terribly painful place.

## ■ MUMMY

When I returned to London in 1961, both Mum and Laurellie came with me. My mother wanted to make sure Laurellie was all set up in the hospital in Kingston for her nursing training. Once she had organised everything and everyone, she returned to Jamaica. She flew back and forth to see her family. These were really the only times she ever travelled; to see her family. She never travelled anywhere for the sake of a holiday or for an adventure. Strong, independent, capable and something of the friendly dragon woman, the only time I ever saw her become coy and shy was when I introduced her to John Richardson and when he flirted with her outrageously. And it worked, because she gave me her blessing to date him.

As Laurellie began to suffer and decline, in the 1970s, May moved to London permanently and bought a flat in Chelsea just two miles from Laurellie. Although May moved to the UK to help Laurellie, Laurellie was equally convinced she helped Mum. Let's say they helped each other then.

When I moved back to London in 1998, the first flat I moved into was in Battersea. The garden had seen better days and required some work and attention. The landlady was an older lady and she sincerely apologised for the state it was in. I might have used that to my advantage in the negotiation stages. Mum was by then 86 years old but she came right over and got stuck in. She ripped out the bushes, hacked back the weeds, chopped down the overgrowth. She was right in there, determined to clear it. I was obsessed with designing my little garden and I turned it into a beautiful tropical wonderland. I built my own pond, with my little fairies surrounding it and of course installed a hammock. It was quite amazing how much I got into that small space. In fact, every time I said I was going to add something, somebody would say, 'Where?' And I just said, 'Watch this space.'

Then, whenever I moved, I would get a bigger place with a bigger garden. Much to my mother's consternation of course, but she would come over and help again to create my banana plantation. She was quite something. And always good fun.

When Laurellie came out of hospital and her health prohibited her from being able to work, she was assigned benefits and accommodation. She was given a nice flat with big rooms on Claverton Street near the river. This was just a half a mile from Mum's place which meant at the weekends, it was easy for her to stay at May's. When I could, I would fly in from LA to see them both. When Laurellie was in hospital, those were the times when Mum would go to Jamaica, or to see me in Rome or LA.

After Laurellie died, Mum and I became very much more inseparable. I introduced her to all my friends and they all fell in love with her. May being the elder to us all, my friends respected that. But that said, she fitted in, she talked to people, she was no little wall flower. She was also the best Christian I have ever met. She was a regular church goer and she was a devoted reader of the bible. This provided her touchstone to the world. Now, being gay is not a big thing in the bible and a lot of my friends are gay, male and female. Very initially I remember her making some comment, not derogatory but it was still something she had noticed and was trying to formalise an impression of, or a way to considering it all. As a devout Christian, this all fell under the 'sin of the people', but as she became further immersed in my friendships, she turned herself and her thinking around for the love of the people. They loved her and she loved them back.

My beloved friends, Stephen Kamlish and Bobby Saunders, who I had met a few months after arriving in London in 1998, and who immediately became my dear friends. They were partners of many years and on meeting Mum, adored her, and she them. It was very sweet when they met each other because Stephen resembled Mum's last boyfriend in Jamaica. So, there was a little gentle flirting which was entirely encouraged by himself. It was so cute.

Steve and Bobby were friends that sat outside of the creative arts and the world of film. Steven was a QC and Bobby was a writer and a journalist. Long term partners of over 30 years. I had known them for about three years when the boys decided to buy and renovate an old farmhouse in Italy. This was in the region of Le Marche in the small province of Ancona in the commune of Serra San Quirico where the cliffs are of limestone, and the villages are medieval.

When the house was completed a couple of years later, they would leave their house in London and take up residence in Italy for three months of the summer. At the beginning of each year, they would call their families and friends, of which there were many and, as the house slept 10, we had to book our dates in. This went on for 15 years. Days would include swimming in the large pool, going on jaunts to discover restaurants or visiting hill-top villages. Evenings would be either dining out or cooking up a feast in the kitchen and serving it on the terrace where we would watch sunsets and moonrises, drink gallons of wine, and share hilarious stories.

Their generosity was limitless and they created the space for so much joy and laughter for us all. They invited my mother to their house but the travel and the terrain around the house was really not conducive to her physical abilities. As I write, they have sold their dream in Italy and have moved to Bath but I will always treasure in my heart the times and the joys and the generosities that the boys included me in as part of their wider reach of tribal gathering.

Hammock bliss for Mummy

I had a couple of lesbian friends who always greeted Mum with big kisses. The couple announced they were going to get married. When she heard about this she said. 'I am going to that.' It was lovely to see her communication and her ways with them. She really bloomed in this respect and I would never think of not including her in all of my plans. She was elegant and proper with a lilting Jamaican accent.

For her 90th, I organised a ladies' lunch for eight people for her birthday at a restaurant.

Mummy and her Queen united on her 100th

For her 100th, I held a catered lunch at my house. There were 30 guests, boys and girls, and some friends provided the catering. I had a friend who did incredible cupcakes; Cupcake Gemma she was called. Instead of one big cake, we laid out a circle of cupcakes. At a certain moment, I presented her with the framed letter from the Queen congratulating her on her 100th. She was absolutely thrilled, because she loved her Queen.

In April 2006, Mum was involved in a leasehold dispute with a freeholder of her little flat in Ifield Road in Chelsea. Demands for large amounts of money for repairs that had never been done just set me on fire, and I found a solicitor who after several months obtained a goodly amount for Mum to be able to rent a flat, which I found for her in Chelsea.

I decided to take her for a little holiday in Truro in Cornwall. We stayed in the Nare Hotel, a luxurious country house right on the beach. She had never had a bloody holiday in her life so I booked it and said, 'We are going on holiday.' We had a large suite, the food was lovely, and it was five days of walking bare foot on the beach. I even treated her to her first facial and massage. I wanted to let her know that all she had done for me was not in vain; taking us to England, taking care of us, being our mummy. Pride and Love showed in her.

Dementia started to creep in when she was around 102. She began repeating herself and it got to the point where she was forgetting things. It's fine, I thought, it's May, she's older. But then one late night, she went on a wander in her dressing gown. The police found her, but I was just freaked. Clearly this was not just about getting older. I took her back to her flat in Chelsea. Still slightly under the effects of being lost, she said she had been looking for her car; a car that she had not had for the last 20 years. The police also came with us to her flat; they were lovely. She 'came back' to us and she had no idea what was happening.

In her proud Jamaican accent she said, 'Why the fuss, what is all this?' 'Darling, you had a wander, and now, you are coming home with me. We are doing this.'

It was getting worse, so we talked to someone about arranging a home for her. She already had some carers, but it had escalated to a new level of danger. After a couple of weeks, I called social care. 'She has to be found a place now. Next time she could be hit by a car.'

In December 2007, I moved her into Christchurch Street and she was happy there until I had to move her into Norbury Hall Care Home; a home dedicated to caring for people suffering from dementia and it was run by an absolutely lovely Indian family. Their daughter, Uma Dhir, who was 30, beautiful and caring, ran the place. The parents I think did the administrative work. I had heard terrible stories about homes and so of course I paid them a visit to have a look around and to speak to the staff. It was lovely. The property sat next to a park, and was surrounded by greenery and trees.

Uma took me on a tour of the home including the room that would be Mum's. The communication and empathy towards the other residents was just lovely, and actually brought me to tears of relief in having found this lovely place.

I held her 103rd birthday at my home and her 104th was organised by the home. For this one, Jeremy Clyde came with me. The staff were so sweet; the home asked me to give them a selection of photographs of her and us and put them together on a display board as a big birthday card. They bought her a cake and made a crown and a sceptre for her to celebrate her royalty within the home.

Myrtle May Penso Beswick died in her sleep two months before her 105th birthday. She had been getting quite frail, she wasn't eating and she had started to go down. All through her decline through dementia, she never forgot my name. There was confusion of course, but not about who I was. I was very grateful for that. She was never aggressive, she was always sweet, and she was always singing.

We didn't have a funeral; instead, we had a cremation. She wanted that. The ashes were sent to me, and Stephen and Bobby took me to the bench in Battersea Park which I had by then already added her name next to Laurellie's. We scattered the ashes with a great deal of laughter as we had to climb over a fence in order to get to the Thames. After that, we were not very elegant. We drank champagne and we told stories. It was a very sweet send-off.

I decided to have a celebration in the garden for 12 people. It was fabulous. When I cleared out her flat, I found that she had been writing her memoirs in long hand on yellow foolscap. The sheets of paper were almost two inches thick. I had no idea she had been doing this. It was fading badly so I copied it all and put it all together in a folder. The memoire was called 'His Daughter Rosie', by May Beswick. It came across as a fictionalised life story, but it was her. She even used some of the words and sentences we had said to each other. Some of it was quite saucy, her talking about all her boyfriends. I had always seen my Mum as proper; however, her memoir made me realise what a passionate woman she had been.

At the garden celebration, I read some of it to the gathering. Mum wrote of Frank Cullen, an Englishman who was in Jamaica for a limited time, 'We were entranced, breathless and infatuated with each other. We knew that was it. Both of us were anticipating the inevitable 'union' '.

Everyone was shocked. 'May', they extolled. 'May Beswick, you saucy thing!'

## HOUSE OF THE GORGON

My first convention in the UK was in late 1998. It was the very one where I met Caroline Munro, her best friend Jayne Crimin, and Shirely Eaton. We all became instant sisters and Jayne, who had been organising the shows for Caroline, asked if I wanted to do them together. I immediately said yes with the stipulation that Jayne had to become my signing agent for 10% commission. Deal sealed.

Doing these shows successively, I began to collate what were soon to become lifelong families and friends. I like to call them my tribes. Caroline's step daughter, Tami Hamalian, began to help with the shows in the US, becoming in effect my stateside agent. She has a big job as a senior paralegal with the coffee shop company, Starbucks. Their headquarters are in Seattle, but she also loves the conventions and got to know many of the people who own and run the shows. She is brilliant, she is organised and she works very much like a producer does. Jayne is my main agent, but for the US, we need Tami. She is also blessed with a very understanding husband who, as soon as he is aware she needs time off for the weekend, he tells her, 'Go, I know you want to have fun. '

Included early on in my tribes was Henry Holland, a retired London tube train driver and a man who just loved his Bond girls, his special ones of whom he would take to lunch. Invariably lasting from 1.30-6.30pm, they quickly became known as Henry Lunches. In attendance was Caroline Munro, Jayne Crimin, Carole Ashby and me. We would get so excited when we set the date because it was always such a treat.

Whenever any of us were invited to a show, we were always very excited to learn who we knew and who we were going to play with. And the making of great connections has really never ended. We were always thrilled our fans want to see us and be with us and in turn that made, and makes, the shows to be true adventures. Caroline and I thrive on the Q&A sessions and there are times when we are almost brought to tears by the tributes we receive from the fans, and for the roles we have played in the films. It really never ceases to blow our minds that so many people are there for us at these shows.

Whenever I would be invited to the US shows, I would meet up with fellow actors for reunions, and a drink or two at the end of the weekend; people such as Adam West, Earl Cameron, Lee Majors, Robert Wagner, Louis Gossett, and the actor and singer, John Leyton.

The thing about these conventions is that there are also always a lot of other things going on; they are not limited to just discussions and signings. As I continued the shows into 2015, I met Mark Statler and his brother, Theron. Singer musicians, they wanted to produce an album to celebrate the Hammer Horror films and their actresses. They set up a studio in a hotel with all the proper recording and mixing equipment and, together with Caroline, Veronica Carlson, Suzanna Leigh and French actress, Yvonne Monlaur, we all sang on separate tracks with Mark's Creepy Classic Chiller Band. They produced the album and it was called Hammer Girls. To this day, I sell them at the conventions.

In 2016, I met actor/writer/director/producer, Mark Redfield at another US convention. Owning Redfield Arts Audio, he and his company produce audio books and audio dramas in Baltimore. Mark had created a story called Sinbad and the Pirate Princess. Sinbad was commanded by his Caliph to rid the Arabian Sea of a ferocious female pirate called Junah and who preys on the ships in the waters of the small island of Zelos as ruled by Queen Badra. Mark suggested I played Queen Badra and Caroline would play Junah in a tale that offered treachery, sorcery, treasure and a blood thirsty sea serpent. Together with four other actors, we flew in five days prior to the convention. We rehearsed for a couple of days and recorded for three days in one of the banquet rooms that had been set up as a recording studio. We had a wonderful time acting in our radio play. I have and sell the CDs too at conventions.

It was in 2013 that I first met Joshua Kennedy. We met at a convention in Newark. Joshua epitomises the definition of an enthusiastic horror film fan. Born in Texas in 1994 and first picking up a film camera at the age of five, he began to create films as extensions of his favourite movies; predominantly the Hammer Horror films. It was from a position of love that his movies were made, often to be funny, but never to parody. Through conversation with him, I saw and understood his driving force. In his words, he likened his process to 'quixotic endeavours'.

From high school, he had gone to Pace University in New York to further study film making. With such a concentration of budding film makers in such a small area, Pace served to become his own personal backlot, providing in the process a much larger canvas upon which to work. Already by then he had become adept at coercing his high school friends into assisting his endeavours. By contrast his fellow students provided much more enthusiasm and time and capability. It was here his fine tuning rapidly increased whereby, he said, he was able to write, produce, direct, act in, edit and showcase a film to premiere in four months; all while attending class and completing exams.

Prior to meeting him, Tami had received an email from Joshua stating he was a huge fan of mine, that he wanted to meet me and was requesting that we make a video together. Tami had met or spoken to him by this time and I whined a bit, 'Do I have to meet him?' 'Just meet him', she pushed back. 'You guys will get on.' And she was right, we absolutely did get on.

In 2014, we met again at the Monster Bash in Mars, Pittsburgh. It was during then that we committed to doing a video together. They were music videos. He picked a song that he thought to be a fitting tribute or subject matter and put together the scenes we would film to the track. With me, and sometimes Caroline, he would star, lead and direct. Invariably top hatted and in costume, between 2014 and 2017 we created four such videos, all of which are still on YouTube.

Aside from Joshua's evident love of film, the genre and, dare I say it, me, it was here that I saw just how utterly prepared he was in every respect. With his confidence of youth and all-round enthusiasm, he would always show up on set, or in a booked hotel suite, completely prepared with his storyboards and blocking ideas. There was absolutely no wasted time. Of these little videos, he later made a book for me; a photo album, with notes of what we did, the songs we sang and where we made them.

It was in 2017 when we met again at the Chiller Convention in New Jersey where he told me he had been thinking about making a movie based on his favourite horror film, *The Gorgon*. He wanted to make it 'with all these lovely ladies.' It would be called *The House of the Gorgon*, another one of his 'extension of' ideas. The lovely ladies would be Caroline Munro, Veronica Carlson and me. He had also approached Christopher Neame, who had played as assistant to Christopher Lee's Dracula in Hammer's Dracula AD and 'Fallon' in the James Bond film, *Licence to Kill*.

The original film, *The Gorgon*, had already by then been inspiration for another of Joshua's films, *The Night of the Medusa*. A year later, he had written the script and sent it to us all. Caroline and I were the evil sisters, Veronica the sweet sister, Caroline's daughter, Georgina 'JoJo' Dugdale, was the film's ingénue and Christopher the protagonist. Of the people who were UK based, we gathered at my place to run through the script and perform initial rehearsals. Even though we had all done other things in TV and film, for this project we were all thoroughly excited and invested. We knew what he could do and we all trusted the fact that he would do it again. So, we were in for it, no question.

In 2019, we all made the journey to Kennedy's home state of Texas. We were all based in a hotel local to where the filming would take place and again, everything was completely organised and efficient. We rehearsed for two days and shot the entire film in eight days.

Joshua had rented the La Antigua Revilla Banquet Hall in Edinburg, Texas. Normally used for graduations, weddings and big celebrations, he had chosen the venue because it also had all the space requisite to a studio shoot; kitchen, restrooms, make-up rooms, and all the space he needed for his sets and set dressing. He had all the costumes waiting for us, the sets were completed; it was all set up for us for when we got there,

Quite simply, it was one of the most enjoyable and most wonderful shoots I have ever been on. In terms of the love and support we gave each other; this filming was a real treasure. We were all completely committed to this. Even when we, the actors, were not required on set, it was impossible for all of us to not be on the set. We were all completely attached to this project. It was a most wonderful experience. Joshua was just 25 at the time.

I think it was the first time he had a real technical crew waiting supporting him to help move sets and props. He had a lighting designer, a sound engineer, a director of photography and a team of assistant directors who worked what turned out to be very long days.

I have no idea from where he gets his backing. We never talked money. I am aware he has relationships with DVD distributors for products once they are ready for showcasing. But, we were all paid. We were taken care of. We were all expensed for flights and a hotel. It was an incredible achievement from someone so young.

Earlier in the book, I had admitted to feeling perfectly happy to retire from acting. The passion had died, and for this business without that cornerstone of feeling, you won't get anywhere. So, why did I say yes to this? In the end, and as far as I am concerned, I would get out of retirement only for him. I found I had no hesitation in agreeing to do this film as I had done all the little videos with him over the preceding few years. Yes, they were small affairs but I had had the opportunity to see the pace at which he worked and how he treated people. I trusted him implicitly to put it together. I knew exactly what we were all getting in to. And because the project included the wider Hammer family, it became a film with family.

It was not just the Hammer girls and Joshua either. Caroline's step daughter, Tami, became the producer of the film. Her organisational skills supported us to get things done. If a wig was not working, she'd sort it.

I had never needed to turn down films in the UK while retired. Although I still have an agent in the UK called Dulcie Huston, the reality is that the phone had stopped ringing. It happens to every actor. Since Joshua's film, a couple of people approached us with ideas but we declined. The point of working with Joshua is because you know you love and know and trust his people. And it was fun. If am not having fun, I am not interested.

The business today is really hard. I have a good friend, Kathy Owen, a Jamaican friend who now lives in Spain. While in Jamaica she was a newsreader, an actor and singer. She married and moved to Spain but whenever she wants to work as an actress, she will come to London and stay with me. For her auditions, I became her assistant, and production and costume designer. Why? Because for auditions today, actors have to make short films and to then send them off to the casting directors. Auditions are now no longer exclusively performed in person. I said to Kathy, 'Bloody hell darling. This business is so alien to me today. I have nothing but great respect for how you are dealing with it.'

And it gets even worse. By way of further example in 2024, she informed me, 'There is a possibility I can do a commercial. I have done some auditions and they want to call me back. But also, could they film it in your house?' What, really? How would anyone feel about that? The initial reaction was of course, 'No', but out of curiosity and help for my friend, I still asked her what was involved. 'Well, they want to shoot through a window over three consecutive night shoots.' My 'No' was building a breadth of shoulder and some antagonism. 'And for whom is this commercial?' 'A big burger chain.'

I was so unutterably angry. How dare they! Sure, they would pay me for it, but to have a bunch of unknown film people in my house for three night-shoots. And it was for the huge hamburger enterprise! What was the most insidious element about this 'audition' was that I was wondering if her getting the part rested on their being able to film in the place of her abode. She was laughing, but she said, 'Yes, that was the deal.'

This is indicative of what I am observing in the industry today. If I were to start again right now, I would be competing with big Oscar winners who are doing TV.

196

So, I would have to start all over again, making my own auditions, editing them and sending them off. No longer really feasible.

If Joshua would ask me again, I would think maybe but I would maybe ask him if he could write the script to omit the longer speeches. Shorter lines and more reactions. I joke a little but mine is a responsibility to the director I now can no longer make. The other thing with Joshua, if we were not sure about something, he would look at us, his hand would go up, and he would say, 'We have oceans of time.' It was with him, a total joy, so calm, I was his muse.

Joshua in the meantime had finished editing the film and, through JoJo's connections within a cinema she worked at, we had the premiere for his film in the Regent Street Cinema in London. This was again an incredible achievement for a micro budget film. Joshua, his team, his parents and family all flew in from Texas. Caroline, Veronica and I invited all of our friends and fans. After the film, we held a Q&A. It was a huge success.

As a result of the success of this premiere, we all became good friends with the cinema's manageress. She was lovely; she thereafter suggested that we would have Sunday screenings of the James Bond films with the Bond girls present. After the film, we would again hold Q&As with Caroline and me. They were a huge success again. It was a success that, after she left working for the cinema, the film and Q&A evening format was retained by the incoming manager with huge stars in attendance such as Steven Spielberg, Emma Stone and Ryan Gosling.

Today, Joshua is a video editor for communities in schools, and a non-profit programme for students who are at risk of dropping out of school. He also teaches philosophy in film at the University of Texas Rio Grande Valley. He is also as I write, doing a musical called Audrey, as inspired by *Little Shop of Horrors*. Every year on his birthday, he watches *Prehistoric Women*. For his 30th birthday in 2024, he wanted to watch the film with me. He flew over to London in June for the weekend and we hung out, wined and dined, laughed a lot and finally took to the sofa together to watch *Prehistoric Women*. Just a perfect weekend.

Gary and Leslie Goeztman, another of my darlings

My last partner,
Steve Counsel, and I
in fancy dress

Steve and Bobby,
two of the most important people in my life

# 12

## CONCLUSION

In terms of reviews for my films, they have been fair to good. However, the one that I really appreciated was for the *Happy Hooker*. In June 1980, Linda Gross of the Los Angeles Times, wrote, 'Beswicke endows Xaviera with class, wit, energy and charm. She plays the madam as a smart business woman who doesn't act coy. When she is tricked, she fights back in kind as a free ethical woman who makes her own choices. When Beswicke says, 'I don't like to be pushed around,' she means it.

I was so thrilled I sent her a huge bouquet of my favourite tropical flowers. She blew me away.

My Life is rich with the deep love I have for my beautiful friends and the love I receive. I suppose I should say I am addicted to love in all its forms. I do not regret that I allowed myself to fall in love, especially with the men in my life. Even if there was always the danger of heartbreak, there was always the deliciousness of that incredible magnetism when one lets go and leaps into the void. Oh joy! Marriage and babies were never in my future and I do not feel like a failure that I have relationships lasting, at most, seven years. I have great admiration for all my friends who have long-term and loving relationships. In terms of woulda coulda shoulda, I can come up with the possibilities in singing and dancing, but I knew that I was obviously not willing to put in the work. And that's ok with me.

How do I want to be remembered? Well, the fact that love is the truest force in my life.

Reunion of best friends, Betty Holtz and Martine

## ◼ ACKNOWLEDGEMENTS

There are so many beautiful people in my life, so many tribes. However, I have to begin somewhere. First and foremost, Simon Firth. Without his listening, his writing, and his immense patience when I incessantly used the word Fun, in my sentences to describe my experiences. But he guided me to tell the stories and indeed to support the use of the aforesaid word for this book.

And then, there is El Presidente, of 007GB Club, Philip Dewhurst, who has been in the background plotting with Simon on where in the world to launch and go with the book.

As you will have noticed, being in love is definitely an addiction for me, and it includes ALL my friends. Many of whom have been included in the stories. But I do have to mention several of those people, starting with those in the USA.

Maud Purcell, Nancy Fasules, Diantha Lebenzon, Gunn Espegard, Lee Kissman, Ken Foree, Luciana Paluzzi and Michael Solomon, Peter and Denise Robinson, Rachel Cora Ward, Stephanie Saunders, Jennifer Spell, Thea Sommer, Irma Singer and Jeffrey Hattanda, Tracy Tynan and Jim McBride, Barbara Steele, Tami and Marc Hamalian, Wes Wheadon, Gary, Leslie, Michael, Eli, Eli Goeztman, and their tribes, Valerie Neale, Barbara Holmes and Tony Friedley, Frank and Sanda Jasper, Sam Irvin, John Logan, Michael Pinzone, Donny and Margaret Cousins, and all my cousins, Arlo Gordin, Camille and Ira Ingber.

My big sister, Faith Baker, in Australia. Kathleen and Skip Heinecke in Ireland.

In the UK, my first family, the Clydes: Jeremy, Jonathan and Pauline, Lucy, Matthew and Beth, Andrew, Toby and Ollie, Tommy and Maddy, Sophie, and Mary Sangster.

Then, Caroline Munro, Jayne Crimin, Carole Ashby, Ronnie Cook, Adrian Fulford and Luis Tejado, Andrea Fettiplace, Gary Stone-Haughton, Gareth and Catherine Humphreys, John and Mandy Warner, Vicki Lewis and Mary George, Lindsay Peebles, Henry Holland, Mel Keen and Julian Richards, Rhianon Tise and Mark Johnson, Edina Ronay and Dick Polak, Graham Rye, John and Pat Symons, Scott Vincent, Marion Wilson.

And to all my amazing Bond sisters; you're just the best.

Please forgive me if I have forgotten anyone and if I have not included their offspring.

Thank you for all the love and support you have given me for the many years, even if we haven't seen each other as regularly as I would have loved to.

Endless love, dear hearts.

## ■ BIOGRAPHY: SIMON FIRTH

Simon Firth became interested in, and subsequently hooked on the world of James Bond when introduced by his father to watch on TV *Dr No* and, months later, *Thunderball*. As a family, the cinematic experience of seeing *The Spy Who Loved Me* left its indelible mark. *Moonraker* further excited and by the time he had seen *For Your Eyes Only*, the focus of his future interests was sealed. An interest in art and marketing saw the creation of a collection of film posters and similar promotional material.

While in awe of the present day's dissection of the subject matter of James Bond into its infinite parts; Clothes, Cars, Food, Drink, Books, Films, Graphic Novels and the multitudinous contributors and content makers plying their knowledgeable and artistic creativity to discuss such, it was for the Bond films' poster artwork that held the greater attraction and subsequent dissection.

Following a love for Villefranche sur Mer and the surrounding countryside's impact on the James Bond films that led to the writing and publication of CÔTE D'AZUR, Simon subsequently wrote and had published the film location-based books, ITALY, FILMING JAMES BOND IN THE BAHAMAS and BOND IN FRANCE. Simon Firth also wrote the words for Jeff Marshall's book, BEAUTY OF BOND.

For all things professional, he is a self-employed contract Project Manager working in the Telecommunications and Media sector.

## ADDITIONAL PHOTO CAPTIONS AND CREDITS

**Page 11** *Thunderball*, 1965, directed by Terence Young. Martine Beswick Luciana Paluzzi and Claudine Auger during a break in filming in the Bahamas; © MGM/Eon Productions/Danjaq

**Page 49** *From Russia with Love* (1963). Sean Connery as James Bond with Martine Beswick, who appears in the film as one of the the fighting gypsy girls, Zora. © Danjaq / MGM, supplied by LMKMEDIA

**Page 50** *From Russia with Love* (1963) promotional photo of Martine Beswick with Sean Connery. Collection Christophel / RnB © Eon Productions / Danjaq

**Page 57** Actress Martine Beswick on the set of *Thunderball* at Pinewood Studios, Buckinghamshire. 12th March 1965 © Mirrorpix

**Page 63** Martine Beswick in a scene from *One Million Years B.C.* © Hammer Film Prod. / 1966 GB © TCD/Prod.DB

Page 64 Martine Beswick & Michael Latimer in *Prehistoric Women* (UK: *Slave Girls*), 25 January 1967 © HAMMER FILMS / Cinematic

**Page 71**  The Beswick Sisters are discovered as a designer and an actress, magazine clipping provided by Martine Beswicke.

**Page 73**  23-year-old Martine Beswick leaves London tonight for Rio, where she will attend the Rio Film Festival promoting the James Bond films. Her 20-year old sister Laurellie made her an exciting wardrobe. Laurellie is currently a nurse but is giving up to be launched into the fashion world as Laurellie Ltd. / 15th September 1965 © Mirrorpix

**Page 84**  Martine Beswick in *Dr Jekyll and Sister Hyde*, directed by Roy Ward Baker (1971) © Hammer Films

**Page 97**  Maurizio and Martine star in *Il Bacio*, in Venice. Martine Beswicke.

**Page 100** The Pantheon in Rome. © Arthousestudio / Pexels

**Page 194** *House of the Gorgon* (2019) by Joshua Kennedy.
Left to right: Caroline Munro, Martine Beswick, Joshua Kennedy, Georgina Dugdale, Veronica Carlson, Christopher Neame. © Gooey Film Productions

**Page 199** Martine Beswick in *Prehistoric Women* (UK: *Slave Girls*), 1967. © HAMMER FILMS

**Page 203** Bond Sisters, always a joy to meet and celebrate!
Top row, left to right: Maud Adams, Caroline Munro, Shirley Eaton, Lana Wood, Luciana Paluzzi, Martine Beswicke, Trina Parks & Priscilla Barnes. Bottom row, left to right: Gloria Hendry & Lynn-Holly Johnson. © Martine Beswicke

www.ingramcontent.com/pod-product-compliance
Lightning Source LLC
Chambersburg PA
CBHW040749150426
42811CB00074B/1955/J